Vocabulary Workshop

Enhanced Edition

The classic program for:

- *developing* and *enhancing* vocabulary resources

- *promoting* more effective communication in today's world

- *improving* vocabulary skills assessed on standardized and/or college-admission tests

By
Jerome Shostak

Sadlier-Oxford

A Division of William H. Sadlier, Inc.
9 Pine Street
New York, NY 10005-1002
1-800-221-5175

5. *see* meaning "to notice" and *see* meaning "the office of a bishop" _____

6. You don't get *down* from a horse, you get *down* from a goose. _____

7. With a sad heart and a most unhappy mind, filled with dire thoughts and deep concern for your welfare, I, nevertheless, for your own well-being, answer your request in the negative. _____

8. fighting with the strength of a thousand men _____

9. as honest as a baby's smile _____

10. the sunshine of your smile _____

III. *In each of the following sentences, encircle the word in parentheses that most satisfactorily completes the meaning.*

1. The term *nerves of steel* has meaning only when it is taken (**literally, figuratively, colloquially**).

2. A type of (**personification, simile, analogy**) commonly found on examinations is "doctor is to hospital as lawyer is to courtroom."

3. "As unpredictable as a day in March" is an expression that is based on a (**metaphor, simile, hyperbole**).

4. The word *lie* meaning "recline" and the word *lie* meaning "falsehood" are (**analogies, homographs, puns**).

5. "We're selling mile-high ice-cream cones" is an example of (**personification, hyperbole, metaphor**).

6. A person who says that he is "ready and willing to help and to be of assistance" is being (**literal, verbose, metaphorical**).

7. "My faith is a rock to which is anchored my happiness" is a sentence based on (**personification, metaphor, simile**).

8. The main character in the fable "The Fox and the Grapes" is a (**metaphor, personification, hyperbole**).

9. "The only way he will ever go up in the world is in an elevator" is an example of a (**pun, colloquialism, personification**) on the words *go up in the world*.

10. In searching for precise language to describe an experiment, a scientist relies on (**verbose, literal, metaphorical**) use of words.

11. Teenagers seem to know many (**figurative, analagous, slang**) expressions that their parents do not understand.

12. Language commonly used in speech or in personal communications, even by educated people, but which would probably be considered unsuitable for formal occasions, is said to be (**colloquial, figurative, personified**).

IV. *The following sentences illustrate use of figurative language. In each case, encircle the expression in the parentheses that most satisfactorily expresses the meaning.*

1. A writer of material for which someone else receives credit is a (**boy who cried wolf, ghostwriter, newshound**).

2. If you approach a person of whom you are somewhat afraid to make a request, you are (**bearding the lion, pulling the wool over that person's eyes, playing the fool**).

3. A person who goes in a vain pursuit of something useless (**has an Achilles' heel, is raising a hue and cry, is on a wild-goose chase**).

4. An item that is of the highest quality is (**way out in left field, of the first water, down in the dumps**).

5. A person who faces difficulties directly and bravely (**takes the bull by the horns, is a wolf in sheep's clothing, is flat on his or her back**).

6. When you do something completely unnecessary, you (**throw out the baby with the bathwater, play it close to the vest, carry coals to Newcastle**).

7. If you begin something at an almost hopeless disadvantage, you are starting out (**with two strikes against you, on cloud nine, in a cloud of smoke**).

8. If you find that no matter what you may do, there is always some special problem or snag to prevent you from reaching your goal, you are a victim of (**catch-22, the catcher in the rye, catch-as-catch can**).

9. A soldier who behaves in a cowardly fashion (**shows the white feather, shoots off his mouth, is a dark horse**).

10. If you want something taken care of promptly, you (**put it on the front burner, ride it into the ground, cry your eyes out**).

11. When two estranged friends settle their differences and take up friendly relations again, they (**are razor sharp, bury the hatchet, lock horns**).

12. A possession that is very costly but proves to be useless is a (**white elephant, hue and cry, pride and joy**).

13. When things are going well for you, (**the goose hangs high, you are eating crow, you are an eager beaver**).

14. When a room is neat and orderly, we say that it is (**up the spout, down the drain, spic-and-span**).

15. A completely unexpected occurrence is called (**the day of the locust, a bolt from the blue, a month of Sundays**).

Diagnostic Test

This Diagnostic Test contains a sampling of the words that are presented in this workbook. It will give you an idea of the types and levels of the words to be studied. When you have completed all the units, the Final Mastery Test will measure your ability to understand and use the words. By comparing your results on the Final Mastery Test with those on the Diagnostic Test below, you will have a basis for judging your progress.

Synonyms

In each of the following groups, encircle the item that best expresses the meaning of the word in **boldface type** in the introductory phrase.

1. assuage her feelings
a. arouse
b. redirect
c. quiet
d. hide

2. elicit a response
a. reject
b. deny
c. explain
d. draw out

3. anonymous rumors and **innuendoes**
a. insinuations
b. lawsuits
c. editorials
d. compliments

4. simulate interest
a. destroy
b. pretend
c. create
d. ignore

5. omit the **lurid** details
a. unimportant
b. repetitious
c. complicated
d. sensational

6. the **epitome** of the scholarly professor
a. embodiment
b. career
c. prestige
d. knowledge

7. nothing but **drivel**
a. nonsense
b. light rain
c. soil
d. pollution

8. precipitated a crisis in the government
a. foresaw
b. prevented
c. analyzed
d. caused

9. commiserate with us
a. sympathize
b. eat
c. discuss
d. travel

10. his **torpid** reactions
a. logical
b. erratic
c. quick
d. sluggish

11. a **propensity** for dangerous pursuits
a. desire
b. inclination
c. distaste
d. dream

12. scurrilous rumors
a. abusive
b. well-informed
c. false
d. interesting

13. abominate all forms of injustice
a. study
b. loathe
c. abolish
d. fear

14. flout her expressed wishes
a. ignore
b. obey
c. back up
d. dislike

15. transient interests
a. long-lasting
b. ardent
c. scholarly
d. temporary

16. unwieldy packages
a. valuable
b. bulky
c. light
d. unidentified

17. an **anomalous** situation
a. safe
b. dangerous
c. embarrassing
d. abnormal

18. the **soporific** effect of the drug
a. narcotic   b. hallucinogenic   c. stimulant   d. laxative

19. **concoct** a story
a. listen to   b. expose   c. make up   d. confirm

20. suffer from **ennui**
a. boredom   b. fever   c. tension   d. fear

21. **heinous** deeds
a. charitable   b. wicked   c. childish   d. effective

22. **castigate** the students
a. address   b. appeal to   c. listen to   d. rebuke

23. order them to **desist**
a. leave   b. fight   c. stop   d. clean up

24. an **infraction** of a regulation
a. violation   b. enactment   c. enforcement   d. author

25. **conducive** to our well-being
a. injurious   b. helpful   c. essential   d. irrelevant

26. **expurgate** a play
a. analyze   b. censor   c. produce   d. develop

27. a state of **bedlam**
a. discipline   b. dreaminess   c. disorder   d. peace

28. **impugn** my sincerity
a. praise   b. question   c. describe   d. imitate

29. remain **irresolute**
a. wavering   b. determined   c. uncontrolled   d. alert

30. a **modicum** of good sense
a. result   b. jot   c. lack   d. trait

Antonyms   *In each of the following groups, encircle the item that means the **opposite** of the word in **boldface type** in the introductory phrase.*

31. the **grisly** scene that met our eyes
a. curious   b. delightful   c. bloody   d. unexpected

32. had a **deleterious** effect on his health
a. harmful   b. puzzling   c. minimal   d. beneficial

33. a decidedly **insular** upbringing
a. foreign   b. narrow   c. cosmopolitan   d. inferior

34. will certainly **buttress** our case
a. undermine   b. clarify   c. clinch   d. strengthen

35. **extraneous** data
a. accurate   b. relevant   c. complete   d. new

36. **corroborate** their testimony
a. report   b. confirm   c. collect   d. refute

37. **covert** meetings
a. occasional   b. noisy   c. public   d. important

38. foment an insurrection
  a. instigate   b. join   c. suppress   d. predict

39. a truly **perceptive** critic
  a. undiscriminating   b. well-known   c. self-appointed   d. shrewd

40. pretentious claims
  a. extravagant   b. meaningless   c. ancient   d. modest

41. a life of **penury**
  a. deprivation   b. opulence   c. sacrifice   d. self-denial

42. paraphrase the passage
  a. consider   b. quote   c. edit   d. publish

43. a truly **inauspicious** beginning
  a. unpromising   b. belated   c. harrowing   d. propitious

44. a **gauche** remark
  a. tactful   b. silly   c. typical   d. pointed

45. a **sleazy** hotel
  a. elegant   b. quaint   c. sordid   d. modern

46. abet the culprits
  a. hinder   b. assist   c. release   d. try

47. her rather **austere** taste in clothing
  a. dreadful   b. flamboyant   c. expensive   d. simple

48. deplete our grain reserves
  a. exhaust   b. commandeer   c. estimate   d. replenish

49. hypothetical situations
  a. interesting   b. typical   c. puzzling   d. actual

50. a **succinct** account of her travels
  a. long-winded   b. simpleminded   c. good-natured   d. lighthearted

Unit 1

Definitions *From the words in Group A and Group B following, choose the one that most nearly corresponds to each definition below. Write the word on the line at the right of each definition and in the illustrative phrase below it.*

Group A

approbation (ap rə 'bā shən)
assuage (ə 'swāj)
coalition (kō ə 'lish ən)
decadence ('de kə dəns)
elicit (ē 'lis it)

expostulate (ik 'späs chə lāt)
hackneyed ('hak nēd)
hiatus (hī 'ā təs)
innuendo (in yü 'en dō)
intercede (in tər 'sēd)

1. (v.) to plead on behalf of someone else; to serve as a third party or go-between in a disagreement _____

   asked me to _____ with the coach on his behalf

2. (adj.) used so often as to lack freshness or originality _____

   a dull and _____ plot

3. (n.) the expression of approval or favorable opinion, praise; official approval or sanction _____

   greeted by smiles of _____

4. (n.) a hint, indirect suggestion, or reference (often in a derogatory sense) _____

   tarnished my reputation by _____

5. (n.) a combination, union, or merger for some specific purpose _____

   a(n) _____ of many community organizations

6. (v.) to draw forth, bring out from some source (such as another person) _____

   attempt to _____ information

7. (n.) a gap, opening, break (in the sense of having an element missing) _____

   puzzled by the _____ in his story

8. (v.) to make easier or milder, relieve; to quiet, calm; to put an end to, appease, satisfy, quench _____

   _____ her hurt feelings

9. (n.) decline, decay, or deterioration; a condition or period of decline or decay; excessive self-indulgence _____

   an example of _____ in modern painting

10. (v.) to attempt to dissuade someone from some course or decision by earnest reasoning _____

   found it useless to _____ with the stubborn referee

Group B

jaded (′jā did)	**provincial** (prə ′vin shəl)
lurid (′lür əd)	**simulate** (′sim yə lāt)
meritorious (mer i ′tôr ē əs)	**transcend** (tran ′send)
petulant (′pech ə lənt)	**umbrage** (′əm brəj)
prerogative (prē ′räg ə tiv)	**unctuous** (′əŋk chü əs)

11. (v.) to make a pretense of, imitate; to show the outer signs of

       to _____ interest in her problems

12. (adj.) wearied, worn-out, dulled (in the sense of being satiated by excessive indulgence)

       _____ from too many parties

13. (n.) foliage giving shade; shade cast by trees; an overshadowing influence or power; offense, resentment; a vague suspicion

       took _____ at such vile treatment

14. (n.) a special right or privilege; a special quality showing excellence

       the _____ of a veteran employee

15. (adj.) causing shock, horror, or revulsion; sensational; pale or sallow in color; terrible or passionate in intensity or lack of restraint

       spare us the _____ details

16. (v.) to rise above or beyond, exceed

       ideas that _____ our comprehension

17. (adj.) pertaining to an outlying area; local; narrow in mind or outlook, countrified in the sense of being limited and backward; of a simple, plain design that originated in the countryside; (n.) a person with a narrow point of view; a person from an outlying area; a soldier from a province or colony

       amused by their _____ manners

18. (adj.) peevish, annoyed by trifles, easily irritated and upset

       will not indulge the _____ child

19. (adj.) fatty, oily, and pliable; excessively smooth or smug; trying too hard to give an impression of earnestness, sincerity, or piety

       offended by his _____ manner

20. (adj.) worthy, deserving recognition and praise

       rewarded after many years of _____ service

Completing   *From the words for this unit (Group A or Group B),*
the Sentence   *choose the one that best completes each of the*
following sentences. Write the word in the space
provided.

1. Various insects have a marvelous capacity to protect themselves by

   _____ the appearance of twigs and other objects in their
   environment.

2. Of course you have a right to ask the waiter for a glass of water, but is

   there any need to use the _____ tone of a spoiled child?

3. I take no _____ at your personal remarks, but I feel you
   would have been better advised not to make them.

4. I feel that, as an old friend, I have the _____ of criticizing
   your actions without arousing resentment.

5. The midnight fire in our apartment building cast a(n) _____ ,
   unearthly light on the faces of the firefighters struggling to put it out.

6. If you take pride in expressing yourself with force and originality, you

   should not use so many _____ phrases.

7. In an age when the United States has truly global responsibilities, we

   cannot afford to have leaders with _____ points of view.

8. In the question-and-answer session, we tried to _____ from
   the candidates some definite indication of how they proposed to reduce
   the national debt.

9. If you cannot meet the college's entrance requirements, it will be futile to

   have someone _____ in your behalf.

10. His confidence grew as he received clear signs of the _____
    of his superiors.

11. The issue of good faith that your conduct raises far _____
    the specific question of whether or not you are responsible for the problem.

12. I certainly appreciate your praise, but I must say that I can see nothing so

    remarkably _____ in having done what any decent person
    would do.

13. When we played back the crucial tape, we realized that there was a(n)

    _____ of several minutes' duration that prevented us from
    understanding what had happened.

14. I like the salespeople in that store because they do their jobs efficiently and

    pleasantly, without making a big show of _____ courtesy.

15. Since I don't like people who play favorites in the office, I have frequently

    _____ against such behavior with my superiors.

16. Their tastes have been so _____ by luxurious living that they seem incapable of enjoying the simple pleasures of life.

17. The only way to defeat the party in power is for all the reform groups to form a(n) _____ and back a single slate of candidates.

18. Weakened militarily, and with a large part of the population living on free "bread and circuses," the once mighty Roman Empire now entered a period of _____ .

19. The manager expressed her unfavorable opinion of the job applicant by _____ rather than by direct statement.

20. Although we tried to express our sympathy, we knew that mere words could do nothing to _____ her grief.

Synonyms   *From the words for this unit (Group A or Group B), choose the one that is most nearly **the same** in meaning as each of the following groups of expressions. Write the word on the line provided at the right.*

1. to feign, pretend, affect   _____

2. an alliance, league, federation, combine   _____

3. to surpass, exceed, outstrip   _____

4. an insinuation, hint, intimation   _____

5. offense, irritation, pique, annoyance   _____

6. narrow-minded, parochial, insular; local   _____

7. oily, mealy-mouthed, servile, fawning   _____

8. sated, satiated, surfeited, cloyed   _____

9. a special right; a perquisite   _____

10. to mitigate, alleviate; to appease, slake, allay   _____

11. a gap, break, lacuna; a pause   _____

12. to intervene, mediate, plead   _____

13. to call forth, evoke, extract, educe   _____

14. banal, trite, commonplace, corny   _____

15. gruesome, gory, grisly; baleful, ghastly   _____

16. decline, decay, degeneration   _____

17. to protest, remonstrate, complain   _____

18. praiseworthy, laudable, commendable _____

19. praise, approval, commendation _____

20. irritable, peevish, testy, waspish _____

Antonyms From the words for this unit (Group A or Group B), choose the one that is most nearly **opposite** in meaning to each of the following groups of expressions. Write the word on the line provided at the right.

1. even-tempered, placid, serene; amiable _____

2. to repress, quash, squelch, stifle _____

3. blameworthy, reprehensible, discreditable _____

4. a splinter group _____

5. cosmopolitan, catholic, broad-minded _____

6. a direct statement _____

7. pleasure, delight, satisfaction _____

8. new, fresh, novel, original _____

9. unspoiled, undiminished, uncloyed _____

10. to intensify, aggravate, exacerbate _____

11. a continuity, continuation _____

12. rise, growth, development, maturation _____

13. disapproval, condemnation, censure _____

14. to remain on the sidelines, stay out of _____

15. pleasant, attractive, appealing; wholesome _____

16. gruff, blunt, bluff _____

17. to be comprehended by, be embraced by _____

Choosing the Right Word Encircle the **boldface** word that more satisfactorily completes each of the following sentences.

1. When the (**umbrage, hiatus**) in the conversation became embarrassingly long, I decided that the time had come to serve the sandwiches.

2. To impress her newly made friends, she (**simulated, assuaged**) an interest in modern art, of which she knew nothing.

3. I see no point in (**expostulating, simulating**) with a person who habitually refuses to listen to reason.

4. Apparently mistaking us for the millionaire's children, the hotel manager overwhelmed us with his (**petulant, unctuous**) attentions.

5. Don't allow yourself the luxury of feeling a sense of (**umbrage, hiatus**) at your supervisor's criticism unless you can afford to quit the job.

6. Ms. Mizote is so accomplished a teacher that she can (**simulate, elicit**) some degree of interest and attention from even the most withdrawn children.

7. The magnificence of the scene far (**simulated, transcended**) my ability to describe it in words.

8. His skillful use of academic jargon and fashionable catchphrases could not conceal the essentially (**hackneyed, meritorious**) quality of his ideas.

9. How can you accuse me of employing (**umbrage, innuendo**) when I am saying in the plainest possible language that I think you're a crook?

10. If you give in to children whenever they cry or whine, you are actually rewarding them for being (**petulant, meritorious**).

11. If you try to (**elicit, intercede**) in a lovers' quarrel, the chances are that you will only make things worse.

12. The American two-party system almost always makes it unnecessary to form a (**hiatus, coalition**) of minority parties to carry on the government.

13. Perhaps it will (**expostulate, assuage**) your fright if I remind you that everyone must have a first date at some time in his or her life.

14. They try to "prove" the (**umbrage, decadence**) of modern youth by emphasizing everything that is bad and ignoring whatever is good.

15. Popularity polls seem to be based on the mistaken idea that the basic task of a political leader is to win immediate (**approbation, coalition**) from the people.

16. I truly dislike the kind of sensational popular biography that focuses solely on the more (**lurid, hackneyed**) or scandalous aspects of a superstar's career.

17. We cannot know today what sort of accent Abraham Lincoln had, but it may well be that there was a decidedly (**meritorious, provincial**) twang in his speech.

18. Anyone who thinks that it is still a gentleman's (**prerogative, hiatus**) to ask a lady to dance didn't attend our Senior Prom.

19. After watching four TV football games on New Year's Day, I was (**jaded, hackneyed**) with the pigskin sport for weeks to come.

20. The most (**meritorious, lurid**) form of charity, according to the ancient Hebrew sages, is to help a poor person to become self-supporting.

Unit 2

Definitions   *From the words in Group A and Group B following, choose the one that most nearly corresponds to each definition below. Write the word on the line at the right of each definition and in the illustrative phrase below it.*

Group A

ameliorate (ə 'mēl yə rāt)
aplomb (ə 'pläm)
bombastic (bäm 'bas tik)
callow ('kal ō)
drivel ('driv əl)

epitome (ē 'pit ə mē)
exhort (eg 'zôrt)
ex officio (eks ə 'fish ē ō)
infringe (in 'frinj)
ingratiate (in 'grā shē āt)

1. (*adj., adv.*) by virtue of holding a certain office   _____

　　called upon to serve _____ as a member of the board

2. (*v.*) to violate, trespass, go beyond recognized bounds   _____

　　inclined to _____ on my area of responsibility

3. (*adj.*) without feathers; without experience; immature, not fully developed; lacking sophistication and poise   _____

　　annoyed by the chatter of _____ young people

4. (*v.*) to improve, make better, correct a flaw or shortcoming   _____

　　took steps to _____ the poor working conditions

5. (*adj.*) pompous or overblown in language; full of high-sounding words intended to conceal a lack of ideas   _____

　　a(n) _____ speech with no solid content

6. (*v.*) to make oneself agreeable and thus gain favorable acceptance by others (sometimes used in a critical or derogatory sense)   _____

　　tried to _____ himself with his superiors

7. (*n.*) a summary, condensed account; an instance that represents a larger reality   _____

　　the very _____ of chivalry

8. (*n.*) poise, assurance, great self-confidence; perpendicularity   _____

　　handled the situation with _____

9. (*v.*) to urge strongly, advise earnestly   _____

　　_____ the team members to make a supreme effort

10. (*n.*) saliva or mucus flowing from the mouth or nose; foolish, aimless talk or thinking; nonsense; (*v.*) to let saliva flow from mouth; to utter nonsense or childish twaddle; to waste or fritter away foolishly   _____

　　to sound like so much _____

Group B

interloper ('in tər lōp ər)
intrinsic (in 'trin sik)
inveigh (in 'vā)
lassitude ('las ə tüd)
millennium (*pl.*, **millennia**)
   (mə 'len ē əm)

occult (ə 'kəlt)
permeate ('pər mē āt)
precipitate (*v.*, pri 'sip ə tāt;
  adj., n., pri 'sip ət ət)
stringent ('strin jənt)
surmise (sər 'mīz)

11. (*v.*) to make a violent attack in words, express
strong disapproval

   _____ against the plan

12. (*v.*) to think or believe without certain supporting
evidence; to conjecture or guess;
(*n.*) an idea or thought that seems likely but lacks
definite proof

   _____ that she would not accept my invitation

13. (*adj.*) belonging to someone or something by its
very nature, essential, inherent; originating in a
bodily organ or part; good for its own sake

   a book with little _____ interest

14. (*adj.*) mysterious, magical, supernatural; secret,
hidden from view; not detectable by ordinary
means; (*v.*) to hide, conceal; eclipse; (*n.*) matters
involving the supernatural

   claiming to have _____ powers

15. (*v.*) to fall as moisture; to cause or bring about
suddenly; to hurl down from a great height; to give
distinct form to; (*adj.*) characterized by excessive
haste; (*n.*) moisture; the product of an action
or process

   the crisis that _____ the war

16. (*n.*) weariness of body or mind, lack of energy

   overcome by _____

17. (*n.*) a period of one thousand years; a period of
great joy, prosperity, or peace

   not spoken in over a(n) _____

18. (*v.*) to spread through, penetrate, soak through

   a driving rain that _____ every bit of clothing

19. (*adj.*) strict, severe; rigorously or urgently binding or
compelling; sharp or bitter to the taste

   more _____ laws against speeding

20. (*n.*) an intruder, one who moves in where he or
she is not wanted or has no right to be

   resented as a(n) _____

Completing the Sentence *From the words for this unit (Group A or Group B), choose the one that best completes each of the following sentences. Write the word in the space provided.*

1. The mere fact that we cannot explain at the present time how she was hurt doesn't mean that she was the victim of some _____ power.

2. "The rash and _____ actions of that young hothead almost cost us the battle, to say nothing of the war," the general remarked sourly.

3. "If you think my training rules are too _____ and confining," the coach said, "then you probably shouldn't be a candidate for the team."

4. Though fossils show that human beings have been on earth a very, very long time, the earliest written records of their activities date back only about five _____ .

5. He tries to give the impression of being a true man of the world, but his conduct clearly shows him to be a(n) _____ and somewhat feckless youth.

6. The Vice President of the United States, the Secretary of State, and the Secretary of Defense are _____ members of the National Security Council.

7. After completing those long, grueling exams, I was overwhelmed by a(n) _____ so great that I felt I would never be able to study again.

8. We do not know what her motives were, but we may _____ that she was concerned mainly for the child's well-being.

9. He has a great deal to say on the subject, but unfortunately most of it is meaningless _____ .

10. We looked up hungrily as the delightful odor of broiled steak and fried onions _____ the room.

11. The voters of this city are looking for practical answers to urgent questions and will not respond to that kind of _____ and pretentious claptrap.

12. The prophets of old fervently _____ the people to amend their lives and follow the path of righteousness.

13. I refuse to accept the idea that conditions in this slum have deteriorated so far that nothing can be done to _____ them.

14. Addressing the school assembly for the first time was a nerve-racking experience, but I managed to deliver my speech with a reasonable amount of _____ .

15. Lucy no doubt is an attractive girl, but isn't it going rather far to call her "the very _____ of feminine beauty and grace"?

16. A good definition of *freedom* is: "The right to do anything you wish as long as you do not _____ on the rights of others."

17. Representing an organization of senior citizens, the rally's keynote speaker _____ vehemently against conditions that rob the elderly of their dignity and independence.

18. The people trying to "crash" our dance may think of themselves as merry pranksters, but they are really _____ who would prevent us all from having a good time.

19. This old necklace has little _____ value, but it means a great deal to me because it belonged to my mother.

20. How can we have any respect for people who try to _____ themselves with their superiors by flattery and favors?

Synonyms   *From the words for this unit (Group A or Group B), choose the one that is most nearly* **the same** *in meaning as each of the following groups of expressions. Write the word on the line provided at the right.*

1. fatigue, lethargy, torpor, languor _____

2. an inference, presumption; to infer, gather _____

3. reckless, impetuous; to provoke, produce _____

4. stern, rigorous, tough; urgent, imperative _____

5. a chiliad; a "golden age" _____

6. to urge, entreat, implore, adjure _____

7. supernatural; esoteric, abstruse; concealed _____

8. immature, inexperienced, green, raw _____

9. to pervade, suffuse, saturate _____

10. to rail, harangue, fulminate, remonstrate _____

11. to encroach, impinge, intrude, poach _____

12. twaddle, tommyrot, balderdash, hogwash; slaver _____

13. inflated, pompous, highfalutin, high-flown _____

14. an intruder, meddler, buttinsky _____

15. an abstract, digest; a model, archetype _____

16. by virtue of one's job _____

17. to cozy up to, curry favor with _____

18. to better, improve, amend _____

19. essential, inherent, immanent, organic _____

20. poise, assurance, confidence, composure _____

Antonyms   *From the words for this unit (Group A or Group B), choose the one that is most nearly **opposite** in meaning to each of the following groups of expressions. Write the word on the line provided at the right.*

1. mature, grown up; polished, sophisticated _____

2. to discourage, advise against, deprecate _____

3. lenient, mild, lax, permissive _____

4. to talk sense; trenchant comments _____

5. to worsen, aggravate, exacerbate _____

6. unadorned, simple, plain, austere _____

7. a rightful member or participant _____

8. mundane; common, public, exoteric _____

9. wary, cautious, circumspect _____

10. to stay in bounds _____

11. to humiliate oneself, mortify oneself _____

12. a proven fact, a certainty _____

13. doomsday, day of judgment _____

14. energy, vitality, animation, liveliness _____

15. confusion, embarrassment, abashment _____

16. extrinsic, external, outward _____

Choosing the Right Word   *Encircle the **boldface** word that more satisfactorily completes each of the following sentences.*

1. A sour odor of decay, stale air, and generations of living (**permeated, precipitated**) every corner of the old tenement.

2. "Long periods of intense boredom punctuated by short periods of intense fear"—in this famous definition a British general (**epitomized, infringed**) the nature of war.

3. In this situation we cannot act on the basis of what may be (**surmised, inveighed**) but only in accordance with what is definitely known.

4. Do we need new laws to combat crime, or rather, more (**ingratiating, stringent**) enforcement of the laws we already have?

5. Because I believe in spreading governmental powers among several officials, I am opposed to having the Mayor serve (**occult, ex officio**) as head of the Board of Education.

6. When the bridge suddenly collapsed in the high winds, the people on it at the time were (**inveighed, precipitated**) to their deaths in the watery abyss below.

7. Must we continue to listen to all this childish (**lassitude, drivel**)!

8. I can usually forgive a(n) (**callow, ex officio**) display of feeble jokes and showing off—but not by someone who has passed his 40th birthday!

9. It is easy to (**inveigh, precipitate**) against "dirty politics," but less easy to play a positive role, however small, in the political process.

10. There is evidence which proves that many persons supposed to possess (**occult, stringent**) powers have either been clever frauds or the victims of self-deception.

11. After the unexpected defeat, the members of the team wanted to be alone and regarded anyone who entered the locker room as a(n) (**interloper, lassitude**).

12. She handled a potentially embarrassing situation with such cool (**drivel, aplomb**) that it passed almost without notice.

13. The song had a pleasant, (**stringent, ingratiating**) melody that gained it quick popularity and then caused it to be forgotten just as quickly.

14. In stating that "All men are created equal and endowed . . . with certain unalienable rights," the. Declaration of Independence proclaims the (**intrinsic, callow**) value of every human being.

15. After years of fighting for social reforms, she experienced a sort of spiritual (**lassitude, aplomb**) that caused her to withdraw and let other people lead the struggle.

16. His message may seem to be (**bombastic, callow**), but there is a solid framework of practical ideas underlying the rather pompous language.

17. We are all ready and willing to do what must be done; what we need is leadership—not (**exhortation, aplomb**)!

18. "I'm sure your every wish will be granted," I assured the demanding child, my tongue firmly in my cheek, "when and if the (**exhortation, millennium**) ever comes!"

19. I trust that we will have the will to improve what can now be improved and the patience to bear what cannot now be (**ameliorated, surmised**).

20. The publisher will take prompt legal action against anyone who (**inveighs, infringes**) on the copyright of this book.

Unit 3

Definitions *From the words in Group A and Group B following, choose the one that most nearly corresponds to each definition below. Write the word on the line at the right of each definition and in the illustrative phrase below it.*

Group A

abominate (ə 'bäm ə nāt)
acculturation (ə 'kəl chə rā shən)
adventitious (ad ven 'tish əs)
ascribe (ə 'skrīb)
circuitous (sər 'kyü ə təs)

commiserate (kə 'miz ə rāt)
enjoin (en 'join)
expedite ('ek spə dīt)
expiate ('ek spē āt)
ferment (n., 'fər ment; v., fər 'ment)

1. (v.) to make amends, atone, make up for; to ward off or avert _____

   willing to _____ her guilt

2. (v.) to make easy, cause to progress faster _____

   _____ the work

3. (v.) to have an intense dislike or hatred for _____

   truly _____ the tactics that terrorists employ

4. (v.) to assign or refer to (as a cause or source), attribute _____

   _____ his fear to insecurity

5. (adj.) resulting from chance rather than from an inherent cause or character; accidental, not essential; (medicine) acquired, not congenital _____

   a(n) _____ meeting that had far-reaching results

6. (v.) to direct or order; to prescribe a course of action in an authoritative way; to prohibit _____

   _____ us to attend the service

7. (v.) to sympathize with, have pity or sorrow for, share a feeling of distress _____

   _____ with them in their mourning

8. (n.) the modification of the social patterns, traits, or structures of one group or society by contact with those of another; the resultant blend _____

   a slow process of _____

9. (adj.) roundabout, not direct _____

   follow a(n) _____ path through the woods

10. (n.) a state of great excitement, agitation, or turbulence;
    (v.) to be in or work into such a state; to produce alcohol by chemical action _____

    caught in the _____ of revolution

Group B

inadvertent (in əd ′vər tənt)
nominal (′näm ə nəl)
noncommittal (nän kə ′mit əl)
peculate (′pek yü lāt)
proclivity (prō ′kliv ə tē)

sangfroid (sän ′frwä)
seditious (sə ′dish əs)
tenuous (′ten yü əs)
vitriolic (vi trē ′äl ik)
wheedle (′whēd əl)

11. (adj.) bitter, sarcastic; highly caustic or biting (like a strong acid) _____

    hurt by his _____ comments

12. (v.) to use coaxing or flattery to gain some desired end _____

    _____ her mother into giving consent

13. (v.) to steal something that has been given into one's trust; to take improperly for one's own use _____

    _____ from the company's retirement fund

14. (n.) a natural or habitual inclination or tendency (especially of human character or behavior) _____

    a(n) _____ for nature study

15. (adj.) existing in name only, not real; too small to be considered or taken seriously _____

    asking only a(n) _____ sum for their services

16. (adj.) resistant to lawful authority; having the purpose of overthrowing an established government _____

    to search out and put down _____ activities

17. (adj.) thin, slender, not dense; lacking clarity or sharpness; of slight importance or significance; lacking a sound basis, poorly supported _____

    the _____ thread of life

18. (adj.) not decisive or definite; unwilling to take a clear position or to say yes or no _____

    confused by her _____ answer

19. (n.) composure or coolness, especially in trying circumstances _____

    behaved with limitless _____

20. (adj.) resulting from or marked by lack of attention; unintentional, accidental _____

    a(n) _____ admission of guilt

3

Completing the Sentence   *From the words for this unit (Group A or Group B), choose the one that best completes each of the following sentences. Write the word in the space provided.*

1. We Americans do not believe that honest criticism of our public officials, no matter how severe, should be regarded as _____ .

2. He claims to be a close friend of the Senator, but I believe that the connection between them is extremely _____ .

3. Since she seems to have a strong _____ both for science and for service to others, I think that she should plan to study medicine.

4. If, as you say, your slamming of the door on the way out was completely _____ , you should be more careful in the future.

5. Wines from that part of France are produced by _____ the juice of the luscious grapes that grow on the hillsides.

6. We had hoped to learn his opinion of the new energy program, but he remained completely _____ during the interview.

7. As charming, clever, and persuasive as she may be, she will certainly not _____ me into lending her my tennis racquet.

8. You could have indicated frankly what you thought was wrong without embittering them with such _____ criticism.

9. The noted humanitarian _____ her audience to play some part, however small, in her great crusade for human betterment.

10. He _____ the crime committed during his youth by a lifetime of service to humanity.

11. His line of questioning was so _____ that I began to suspect that he himself was not sure of what he was trying to prove.

12. Much of the money that the "robber barons" _____ from the public trust was never recovered—or even missed!

13. While he remained the _____ leader of the group, the real power passed into the hands of his wily aide.

14. Some people say that they cannot understand her defeat in the election, but I _____ it to her failure to discuss the issues in simple, down-to-earth terms.

15. Contacts with the modern world may still be infrequent, but the primitive peoples of New Guinea are already showing signs of _____ .

16. No matter what their other likes or dislikes are, all Americans thoroughly _____ slavery in all its forms.

17. We must distinguish between the truly basic policies of our political party and those which are _____ and have little connection with the essential program.

18. Who in the world can hope to match the unshakable _____ of the indestructible James Bond in moments of great peril?

19. Only someone who has suffered from bursitis can fully _____ with me when I am in the throes of an acute attack.

20. The new computerized referral system will greatly _____ the processing of complaints by customers.

21. Declaring the boycott to be illegal, the judge _____ the labor union from applying it against the employing firm.

22. True, the cabdriver took a(n) _____ route to the hotel, but his purpose was to avoid heavy traffic—not to build up the fare.

Synonyms   *From the words for this unit (Group A or Group B), choose the one that is most nearly **the same** in meaning as each of the following groups of expressions. Write the word on the line provided at the right.*

1. to loathe, abhor, despise, detest   _____

2. extrinsic, incidental; fortuitous   _____

3. to accelerate, facilitate, speed up   _____

4. withering, acerbic, mordant, caustic   _____

5. playing it safe, playing it close to the vest   _____

6. slender, flimsy, unsubstantial; vague, hazy   _____

7. to embezzle, defraud, misappropriate   _____

8. indirect, roundabout, meandering   _____

9. to bid, charge, command, adjure   _____

10. a natural bent, penchant, propensity   _____

11. mutinous; rebellious; subversive   _____

12. poise, self-assurance, equanimity   _____

13. to sympathize, feel sorry for, empathize   _____

14. to cajole, inveigle, soft-soap, sweet-talk   _____

15. to atone for, redeem, make amends for   _____

16. adopting ways of another social group   _____

17. titular, token; trifling, inconsequential _____

18. to impute, attribute, credit _____

19. commotion, turmoil, turbulence, unrest _____

20. accidental, unintentional _____

Antonyms　　From the words for this unit (Group A or Group B), choose the one that is most nearly **opposite** in meaning to each of the following groups of expressions. Write the word on the line provided at the right.

1. essential, intrinsic, inherent; congenital _____

2. bland; saccharine, honeyed, sugary _____

3. to relish, savor, cherish, esteem _____

4. straight, direct, as the crow flies _____

5. to hinder, hamper, impede, obstruct _____

6. supportive, loyal, faithful, allegiant _____

7. real, actual; exorbitant, excessive _____

8. excitability, hysteria, flappability _____

9. positive, definite, committed _____

10. peace and quiet, tranquillity, placidity _____

11. a natural disability or incapacity _____

12. deliberate, intentional, premeditated _____

13. strong, solid, substantial, valid _____

14. to coerce, browbeat, intimidate, strong-arm _____

15. to feel no sympathy for _____

Choosing the Right Word　　Encircle the **boldface** word that more satisfactorily completes each of the following sentences.

1. Although that critic is feared for (**noncommittal, vitriolic**) reviews, I have learned that there is usually a sound basis for her unfavorable judgments.

2. Since Alfred has been able to (**expiate, wheedle**) almost anything he wants out of his parents, he is quite unprepared now to face the harsh realities of life.

3. I learned that I would have to make a choice between my strong aversion to hard work and my equally strong (**proclivity, wheedle**) for eating.

4. It is only in my fantasies that I display the (**ferment, sangfroid**) associated with movie heroes who are "as cool as a cucumber."

5. Experienced lawyers know that the line between literal truth and slight but significant distortion of the facts is often a (**seditious, tenuous**) one.

6. Although the Queen is the (**nominal, adventitious**) head of state, the Prime Minister is the real leader of the British government.

7. (**Peculation, Sedition**) was such a common offense among Roman provincial governors that, when asked how they made their fortunes, most simply replied, "In the provinces."

8. The Biblical prophets (**abominated, acculturated**) idol worship of any kind and railed vehemently against such loathsome practices.

9. With the deadline fast approaching, the local newspaper office was in a (**ferment, sedition**) of last-minute activity and preparation.

10. When I spoke to Mother about going on the Easter trip to Washington, her only reply was a (**nominal, noncommittal**) "We'll see."

11. Modern American society can justly be said to be the end point of the (**commiseration, acculturation**) of diverse groups of immigrants.

12. You are following an all too familiar pattern in (**ascribing, expediting**) your failures to anyone and everyone—except yourself.

13. I was simply unable to follow the (**circuitous, adventitious**) reasoning by which she "proved" that a straight line is not necessarily the shortest distance between two points.

14. He is a conscientious objector to military service because he is (**enjoined, ascribed**) by a deep religious conviction not to take a human life.

15. (**Commiseration, Proclivity**) is a noble human emotion, but in itself it is no substitute for vigorous efforts to help other people.

16. His investments proved to be profitable, but I think this was (**adventitious, nominal**) rather than the result of knowledge and planning.

17. An experienced politician always tries to avoid making (**noncommittal, inadvertent**) remarks that may offend some voters.

18. After he had seen the error of his ways, the villain attempted to (**expiate, enjoin**) the dark deeds of his past by acts of kindness and mercy.

19. The worst way I can think of to (**expedite, ascribe**) this program would be to set up a new Committee on (**Expediting, Ascribing**) Programs.

20. Our armed forces are prepared to deal with aggression from outside, but our best defense against (**sedition, peculation**) at home is the deep loyalty of the overwhelming majority of the American people.

21. They insist that they have a real legal interest in those patent rights, but I suspect that their claim is (**tenuous, circuitous**) at best.

22. The (**adventitious, nominal**) membership of that party is very large, but there are only a few thousand people who take an active part in its affairs.

Review Units 1–3

Analogies *In each of the following, encircle the item that best completes the comparison.*

1. nominal is to **exorbitant** as
a. provincial is to parochial
b. bombastic is to occult
c. tenuous is to substantial
d. lurid is to sensational

2. callow is to **experience** as
a. self-assured is to aplomb
b. exhausted is to lassitude
c. petulant is to imagination
d. provincial is to sophistication

3. rant is to **bombastic** as
a. exhort is to jaded
b. whine is to inadvertent
c. inveigh is to vitriolic
d. advocate is to noncommittal

4. hackneyed is to **originality** as
a. circuitous is to direction
b. tenuous is to soundness
c. adventitious is to chance
d. intrinsic is to value

5. meritorious is to **approbation** as
a. noncommittal is to consent
b. reprehensible is to condemnation
c. seditious is to commiseration
d. laudable is to abomination

6. unctuous is to **oil** as
a. vitriolic is to acid
b. decadent is to water
c. petulant is to wine
d. seditious is to milk

7. embezzler is to **peculate** as
a. sovereign is to precipitate
b. critic is to expiate
c. interloper is to infringe
d. engineer is to simulate

8. inadvertent is to **deliberate** as
a. meritorious is to commendable
b. unctuous is to occult
c. petulant is to peevish
d. adventitious is to intrinsic

9. lassitude is to **fatigue** as
a. ingratiation is to senility
b. decadence is to decay
c. acculturation is to paralysis
d. sedition is to decrepitude

10. lax is to **stringent** as
a. circuitous is to straight
b. hackneyed is to trite
c. seditious is to subversive
d. occult is to arcane

11. drivel is to **substance** as
a. criticism is to simplicity
b. gibberish is to meaning
c. reply is to thoroughness
d. adage is to coherence

12. awkward is to **aplomb** as
a. jaded is to decadence
b. brazen is to temerity
c. excitable is to sangfroid
d. militant is to activity

13. assuage is to **irritate** as
a. intercede is to meditate
b. expedite is to hamper
c. surmise is to verify
d. ameliorate is to improve

14. wheedle is to **flattery** as
a. ingratiate is to threats
b. transcend is to prerogatives
c. simulate is to surmises
d. insinuate is to innuendos

15. millennium is to **century** as
a. ton is to pound
b. dollar is to dime
c. hour is to minute
d. meter is to centimeter

16. hiatus is to **gap** as
a. epitome is to synopsis
b. ferment is to tranquillity
c. umbrage is to pleasure
d. proclivity is to dislike

17. expostulate is to **reason** as
a. inveigh is to invective
b. exhort is to compliment
c. permeate is to warning
d. transcend is to argument

18. umbrage is to **resent** as
a. interest is to ascribe
b. notice is to abominate
c. delight is to relish
d. pity is to enjoin

Synonyms   *In each of the following groups, encircle the word or expression that is most nearly **the same** in meaning as the word in **boldface type** in the introductory phrase.*

1. expostulate with the referee
a. argue   b. dine   c. consult   d. travel

2. during the last **millennium**
a. famine   b. world war   c. 1000 years   d. election

3. exhort them to cooperate
a. order   b. encourage   c. help   d. forbid

4. a **prerogative** to change your mind
a. desire   b. refusal   c. privilege   d. necessity

5. took **umbrage** at my remark
a. pleasure   b. offense   c. hint   d. good advice

6. intercede in someone's behalf
a. pay   b. withdraw   c. confirm   d. mediate

7. ascribe the painting to Picasso
a. sell   b. credit   c. deliver   d. offer

8. a period of **decadence**
a. decline   b. prosperity   c. confusion   d. power

9. a **vitriolic** attack
a. mild   b. extremely bitter   c. justified   d. foolish

10. peculated from company funds
a. allotted   b. stolen   c. donated   d. spent

11. infringe on my territory
a. inspect   b. trespass   c. do business   d. travel

12. transcend understanding
a. surpass   b. help   c. expand   d. prevent

13. permeate the air
a. breathe   b. perfume   c. spoil   d. fill

14. simulate his mannerisms
a. imitate   b. make fun of   c. admire   d. dislike

15. stop the **interloper**
a. criminal   b. loudmouth   c. intruder   d. foreigner

16. adopt **stringent** rules
a. lenient   b. unnecessary   c. punitive   d. strict

17. a **lurid** account of the tragedy
a. lively   b. sensational   c. circumspect   d. succinct

18. enjoined our attendance
a. commanded   b. permitted   c. enjoyed   d. paid for

19. a **proclivity** for foreign languages
a. dislike   b. inclination   c. genius   d. mental block

20. elicited our applause
a. forbade   b. acknowledged   c. ignored   d. drew forth

Unit 4

Definitions

From the words in Group A and Group B following, choose the one that most nearly corresponds to each definition below. Write the word on the line at the right of each definition and in the illustrative phrase below it.

Group A

affable ('af ə bəl)
aggrandize (ə 'gran dīz)
amorphous (ə 'môr fəs)
archetype ('är kə tīp)
aura ('ôr ə)
contraband ('kän trə band)

erudite ('er yü dīt)
gossamer ('gäs ə mər)
infer (in 'fər)
inscrutable (in 'skrü tə bəl)
insular ('in syə lər)

1. (*v.*) to increase in greatness, power, or wealth; to build up or intensify; to make appear greater

   worked to _____ his estate

2. (*adj.*) impossible to see through physically; incapable of being understood

   try to fathom her _____ smile

3. (*n.*) an original model after which similar things are patterned; a perfect or typical example

   the _____ of the automobile

4. (*adj.*) scholarly, learned; boorish, pedantic

   a(n) _____ professor

5. (*v.*) to find out by reasoning; to arrive at a conclusion on the basis of thought; to hint, suggest, imply

   can _____ nothing from his behavior

6. (*adj.*) courteous and pleasant, sociable, easy to speak to

   spent much time with our _____ neighbors

7. (*adj.*) shapeless, without definite form; of no particular type or character; without organization, unity, or cohesion

   the _____ body of the amoeba

8. (*adj.*) thin, light, delicate, insubstantial; (*n.*) a very thin, light cloth

   a(n) _____ thread of the finest silk

9. (*n.*) that which surrounds (as an atmosphere); a distinctive air or personal quality

   marked by a special _____ of goodness

10. (*adj.*) relating to, characteristic of, or situated on an island; narrow or isolated in outlook or experience

    too well educated for such _____ views

11. (*n.*) illegal traffic, smuggled goods;
(*adj.*) illegal, prohibited   _____

       the _____ seized by the police

Group B

irrevocable (i 'rev ə kə bəl)   **retrench** (ri 'trench)
propensity (prə 'pen sə tē)   **reverberate** (ri 'vər bə rāt)
querulous ('kwer ə ləs)   **scurrilous** ('skər ə ləs)
remonstrate (ri 'män strāt)   **sedulous** ('sej ə ləs)
repudiate (ri 'pyü dē āt)   **sleazy** ('slē zē)
resilient (ri 'zil yənt)

12. (*adj.*) thin or flimsy in texture; cheap; shoddy, or
inferior in quality or character; ethically low,
mean, or disreputable   _____

      _____ goods

13. (*adj.*) incapable of being changed or called back   _____

      a(n) _____ decision

14. (*adj.*) persistent, showing industry and
determination   _____

      a(n) _____ copier of others people's work

15. (*v.*) to argue or plead with someone against
something, protest against, object to   _____

      _____ with the child

16. (*v.*) to cut down, reduce in scope and cost   _____

      _____ operations because of poor business

17. (*adj.*) able to return to an original shape or form;
able to recover quickly   _____

      a(n) _____ plastic

18. (*v.*) to re-echo, resound; to reflect or be reflected
repeatedly   _____

      _____ across the valley

19. (*adj.*) peevish, complaining, fretful   _____

      a(n) _____ passenger

20. (*v.*) to disown, reject, or deny the validity of   _____

      _____ a statement

21. (*n.*) a natural inclination or bent toward   _____

      a strong _____ for scientific research

22. (*adj.*) coarsely abusive, vulgar or low (especially in
language), foul-mouthed   _____

      a(n) _____ attack on the absent leader

4

Completing the Sentence   *From the words for this unit, choose the one that best completes each of the following sentences. Write the word in the space provided.*

1. The sharp crack of the rifle shot _____ through the hills.

2. Am I to _____ from what you just said that you were not present at the scene of the accident?

3. This jacket is made of a material so _____ that it sheds wrinkles and keeps its shape even when one has worn it for days.

4. He is really insufferable when he gets into one of those _____ moods in which nothing in the world pleases him.

5. If you happen to have a(n) _____ seatmate on a long airplane flight, you may find yourself talking more freely about personal matters than you would under other circumstances.

6. _____ dives full of disreputable and dangerous-looking characters have given the waterfront areas of many cities a bad reputation.

7. As my opponent cited facts and figures without once referring to notes, I became aware of how _____ she was.

8. He used his admittedly remarkable talents only to _____ himself, not to benefit the society that has been so kind to him.

9. I am not going to _____ the ideas and standards by which I have guided my life just because they have become unpopular.

10. The commitment you have made is _____ without the consent of the other party to the agreement.

11. For all practical purposes the British Parliament was the _____ of the various representative assemblies that now exist in the world.

12. When father lost his job, we held a family council to plan how we would _____ on household expenses.

13. Because of her _____ for gossiping, we tried not to let her learn anything about our personal affairs.

14. His attempts to discredit her by belittling her ability and character were nothing more than _____ abuse.

15. Since our efforts to _____ with the factory managers about pollution of the lake have been ineffective, we are now considering legal action.

16. The program he suggested was so barren of guiding ideas and specific proposals that I felt justified in referring to it as _____ .

17. He tried in vain to guess what surprise he might expect next from that _____ power, Lady Luck.

18. Perhaps she had less native ability than some of her classmates, but her powers of concentration and _____ study program enabled her to finish first in the class.

19. While tsarist Russia's vast territories were almost purely continental, the British Empire included numerous _____ possessions.

20. On his combat uniform he wore absolutely no insignia of rank, but he was surrounded with an unmistakable _____ of authority.

21. Under the latest regulations, any shipment of arms to those countries is illegal and may be seized as _____ .

22. The drops of dew sparkled like diamonds on the _____ threads of the spider web.

Synonyms From the words for this unit, choose the one that is most nearly **the same** in meaning as each of the following groups of expressions. Write the word on the line provided.

1. filmy, diaphanous, airy, feathery _____

2. springy, elastic, buoyant, bouncy _____

3. to curtail, reduce, economize _____

4. obscene, filthy; abusive, vituperative _____

5. to re-echo, resound, boom, thunder, rumble _____

6. a model, prototype; a paragon, epitome _____

7. assiduous, tireless, indefatigable _____

8. to reason against, expostulate _____

9. irreversible, unrecallable _____

10. to disavow, disown, abjure, reject _____

11. peevish, petulant, touchy, cranky _____

12. genial, amicable, agreeable, cordial _____

13. narrow-minded, parochial, provincial _____

14. an atmosphere, ambience, air, quality _____

15. profoundly learned, scholarly _____

16. to increase, augment, amplify, enhance, exalt _____

17. impenetrable, incomprehensible, enigmatic _____

18. shapeless, formless, nebulous _____

19. to gather, surmise, presume; guess, speculate _____

20. inferior, chintzy, cheesy, tawdry, tatty _____

21. illegal, illicit, bootleg, unlawful _____

22. a natural bent, proclivity, penchant _____

Antonyms *From the words for this unit, choose the one that is most nearly **opposite** in meaning to each of the following groups of expressions. Write the word on the line provided.*

1. definite, well-defined, clear-cut _____

2. thick, dense, solid, massive _____

3. uncomplaining, stoical; serene, placid _____

4. lackadaisical, listless, indolent, otiose _____

5. surly, cantankerous; dour, inhospitable _____

6. legal, lawful, licit _____

7. catholic, cosmopolitan, liberal _____

8. rigid, stiff, inflexible, unyielding _____

9. superior, first-rate, quality; sturdy _____

10. to reduce, decrease, diminish _____

11. ignorant, uneducated, illiterate _____

12. comprehensible, intelligible, penetrable _____

13. to avow, affirm, aver, avouch _____

14. decorous, seemly, tasteful, dignified _____

15. a natural incapacity or inability _____

16. reversible, changeable _____

17. to expand, increase, augment, magnify _____

Choosing the Right Word *Encircle the **boldface** word that more satisfactorily completes each of the following sentences.*

1. The language he used in his bitter attack on us was so (**amorphous, scurrilous**) that I hesitate even to repeat it.

2. In an age when the world has become a "global village," we cannot afford leaders with (**insular, sedulous**) outlooks.

3. To limit the free expression of unpopular ideas is to (**repudiate, infer**) the basic spirit of the Bill of Rights.

4. Realizing that the cut in my allowance obliged me to (**repudiate, retrench**), I put myself on a rigorous diet of only one banana split a day.

5. The pitiful derelict's only protection against the elements was a cheap overcoat made out of some kind of (**resilient, sleazy**) material that wouldn't keep the cold out in a heat wave.

6. What we really resent is not sensible criticism but nagging that is petty, capricious, and (**querulous, affable**).

7. Throughout his career, the man has emphasized the (**aggrandizement, inscrutability**) of wealth and power at the expense of other values.

8. What a pleasure to talk about old times with so (**affable, erudite**) a companion!

9. I tried to make some sense out of the strange orders he had given us, but his plan and purpose remained utterly (**erudite, inscrutable**).

10. Lucy finally completed her (**querulous, erudite**) term paper, in which she quoted from more than a hundred sources.

11. The musical composition, with no melodic pattern and no well-defined structure of development, seemed (**amorphous, querulous**) to my ear.

12. Am I to (**remonstrate, infer**) from your statement that there would be no point in further negotiations?

13. On the Sabbath, the entire village is immersed in an (**archetype, aura**) of religious devotion that is difficult to convey to outsiders.

14. Since he seems to have no moral standards whatsoever, it would probably be futile to (**infer, remonstrate**) with him about his outrageous behavior.

15. Our determination never to yield to force or the threat of force is firm and (**amorphous, irrevocable**)!

16. In his conservative gray business suit, he looked for all the world like the (**archetype, propensity**) of a Wall Street executive.

17. I think that nothing in Shakespeare is lighter or more delightful than the (**gossamer, aggrandized**) wit and fancy of A Midsummer Night's Dream.

18. Your (**propensity, retrenchment**) for spending more than you can afford will lead to only one result—bankruptcy!

19. Carefully avoiding any attempt at originality, he has fashioned his style on (**sedulous, scurrilous**) mimicry of other, more talented writers.

20. The minister said that Cain's question, "Am I my brother's keeper?" has continued to (**reverberate, infer**) down the ages.

21. When we arrived home we were tired and depressed, but the (**gossamer, resilient**) spirit of youth made things look brighter the next morning.

22. We cannot bar foreign influences from our shores, and we cannot treat unfamiliar ideas as (**aura, contraband**)!

Unit 6

Definitions   From the words in Group A and Group B following, choose the one that most nearly corresponds to each definition below. Write the word on the line at the right of each definition and in the illustrative phrase below it.

Group A

anomalous (ə 'näm ə ləs)
arbiter ('är bə tər)
aspersion (ə 'spər zhən)
bizarre (bi 'zär)
brusque (brəsk)
cajole (kə 'jōl)

castigate ('kas tə gāt)
contrive (kən 'trīv)
demagogue ('dem ə gäg)
disabuse (dis ə 'byüz)
ennui (än 'wē)

1. (adj.) abrupt, blunt, with no formalities   _____

a(n) _____ refusal

2. (n.) a leader who exploits popular prejudices and false claims and promises in order to gain power   _____

the self-serving tactics of a(n) _____

3. (v.) to coax, persuade through flattery or artifice; to deceive with soothing thoughts or false promises   _____

_____ them into doing what I wanted

4. (n.) weariness and discontent from lack of occupation or interest, boredom   _____

a feeling of profound _____

5. (adj.) abnormal, irregular, departing from the usual   _____

to be placed in a(n) _____ position

6. (v.) to plan with ingenuity, invent; to bring about as the result of a scheme or plan   _____

_____ his rival's downfall

7. (v.) to free from deception or error, set right in ideas or thinking   _____

_____ her of that misconception

8. (n.) one having power to decide a matter at issue; a judge, umpire   _____

the sole _____ of the dispute

9. (adj.) extremely strange, unusual, atypical   _____

a(n) _____ costume

10. (v.) to punish severely; criticize severely   _____

_____ the unruly students

11. (n.) a damaging or derogatory statement; the act of slandering or defaming   _____

cast _____ on my reputation

Group B

fetter ('fet ər)	**surreptitious** (sər əp 'tish əs)
heinous ('hā nəs)	**transgress** (tranz 'gres)
immutable (i 'myü tə bəl)	**transmute** (tranz 'myüt)
insurgent (in 'sər jənt)	**vicarious** (vī 'kâr ē əs)
megalomania (meg ə lō 'mā nē ə)	**vouchsafe** (vaùch 'sāf)
sinecure ('si nə kyür)	

12. (v.) to give or furnish condescendingly; to grant   _____

     reluctant to _____ a reply

13. (n.) a delusion marked by a feeling of power, wealth, talent, etc., far in excess of reality   _____

     prone to feelings of _____

14. (adj.) stealthy, secret, intended to escape observation; made or accomplished by fraud   _____

     a(n) _____ glance

15. (v.) to change from one nature, substance, or form to another; to transform   _____

     hate _____ into love

16. (adj.) not subject to change, constant   _____

     the _____ laws of the universe

17. (v.) to go beyond a limit or boundary; to sin, violate a law   _____

     _____ the divine law

18. (adj.) very wicked, offensive, hateful   _____

     horrified by the _____ crime

19. (n.) one who rebels or rises against authority; (adj.) rising in revolt, refusing to accept authority; surging or rushing in or on   _____

     moved to crush the _____ forces

20. (n.) a chain or shackle placed on the feet (often used in plural); anything that confines or restrains; (v.) to chain or shackle; to render helpless or impotent   _____

     place _____ on each prisoner

21. (n.) a position requiring little or no work; an easy job   _____

     little more than a(n) _____

22. (adj.) performed, suffered, or otherwise experienced by one person in place of another   _____

     in search of _____ excitement

Completing the Sentence   *From the words for this unit, choose the one that best completes each of the following sentences. Write the word in the space provided.*

1. Anyone who refers to my job as a(n) _____ should spend just one day in my place!

2. The speaker's blatant appeal to the emotions of the crowd smacked more of the _____ than the true leader of the people.

3. Although most of us lead a quiet, humdrum sort of life, we can all get a(n) _____ thrill from the achievements of our astronauts.

4. The _____ way in which they planned the undertaking shows that they were aware of its illegal character.

5. I welcome honest criticism, but I resented deeply their _____ on my sincerity and good faith.

6. In his determination to be blunt and honest, he has _____ the limits of good taste.

7. How can we be at the airport to meet her when her secretary will not _____ any information about her time of arrival?

8. The Emancipation Proclamation issued by Abraham Lincoln once and for all broke the _____ that bound Southern blacks to a life of servitude and humiliation.

9. Is there any other crime in history as _____ as the attempt of the Nazis to annihilate so-called "inferior" racial groups?

10. Resorting to rather farfetched promises, I finally _____ Tina into going to the prom with me.

11. Although the _____ were defeated by the government's forces, a small group escaped into the mountains, where they kept alive the spirit of rebellion.

12. After the reporters had submitted detailed questions to the Governor, they were annoyed by his _____ answer, "No comment."

13. Whenever we disagree over which TV program to watch, my father serves as a(n) _____ by selecting the program *he* wants.

14. His conceit is so great and so immune to the lessons of experience that it must be considered a kind of _____ .

15. The alchemists of the Middle Ages, who were both skilled magicians and primitive chemists, hoped to _____ base metals into gold.

16. At the very outset of the term, I urged you to _____ yourself of the idea that you can pass this course without hard, regular work.

17. Wearing _____ masks at Halloween is a tradition that goes back many centuries.

18. The one fact about nature that seems completely _____ is that everything in nature is subject to change.

19. His endless talk about himself and his interests is truly unexcelled for producing _____ in others.

20. I find it hard to understand how they were able to _____ such an elaborately underhanded scheme in so short a time.

21. Since he had always been quiet and retiring, we were amazed when he stood up at the meeting and _____ the chairperson for failing to give everyone a chance to speak.

22. Can you imagine anything as _____ as a successful drama coach who has never acted on the stage!

Synonyms *From the words for this unit, choose the one that is **the same** in meaning as each of the following groups of expressions. Write the word on the line given.*

1. to convert, translate, metamorphose _____

2. to concede, deign, bestow, confer; to permit _____

3. delusions of grandeur _____

4. languor, world-weariness, listlessness _____

5. a "no-show" job, cushy job, "plum" _____

6. surrogate, substitute; imagined, secondhand _____

7. a rabble-rouser, firebrand _____

8. an innuendo, slander, calumny, denigration _____

9. to chastise, rebuke, censure, upbraid _____

10. furtive, clandestine, covert, concealed _____

11. grotesque, fantastic, outlandish _____

12. curt, tactless, ungracious, rough _____

13. evil, odious, abominable, outrageous _____

14. to overstep, exceed, trespass; to err _____

15. rebellious, mutinous; a revolutionary _____

16. to think up, devise, concoct, fabricate _____

17. to undeceive, enlighten, set straight _____

18. unchangeable, unalterable, fixed, invariable _____

19. a referee, arbitrator, mediator; an authority _____

20. to wheedle, inveigle, softsoap, sweet-talk _____

21. exceptional, atypical, unusual, aberrant _____

22. a bond, restraint; to bind, restrain, hamper _____

Antonyms *From the words for this unit, choose the one that is most nearly **opposite** in meaning to each of the following groups of expressions. Write the word on the line given.*

1. gracious, tactful, courteous, diplomatic _____

2. changeable, inconstant; variable; fickle _____

3. to free, liberate, emancipate _____

4. real, actual, firsthand _____

5. normal, regular, customary, typical, ordinary _____

6. an endorsement, testimonial; praise _____

7. to obey, toe the line _____

8. to maintain unchanged, preserve _____

9. open, frank, aboveboard, overt _____

10. enthusiasm, liveliness, excitement, intensity _____

11. to deceive, delude, pull wool over one's eyes _____

12. to withhold, deny _____

13. loyal, faithful; a loyalist _____

14. humility, modesty, self-abasement _____

15. a high-pressure job, challenge _____

16. to coerce, force, strongarm _____

Choosing the Right Word *Encircle the **boldface** word that more satisfactorily completes each of the following sentences.*

1. Although her new position bore a high-sounding title, it was really little more than a(n) (**insurgent, sinecure**).

2. The institutions of our society, far from being (**immutable, anomalous**), are in the process of change at this very moment.

3. He may have kept within the letter of the law, but there is no doubt that he has (**cajoled, transgressed**) the accepted moral code.

4. With the innumerable activities open to a young person like you, I can't understand why you should suffer from (**ennui, megalomania**).

5. Her description of the Western frontier was so vivid that I seemed to be experiencing (**vicariously, surreptitiously**) the realities of pioneer life.

6. By casting (**sinecures, aspersions**) on the ability and character of others, you reveal the misgivings you have about yourself.

7. I cannot understand how she was able to (**disabuse, contrive**) a meeting between two people who had flatly refused to meet each other.

8. His authority in deciding matters of good taste was so widely recognized that he became known as the "(**Arbiter, Aspersion**) of Elegance."

9. Have you ever heard of anything as (**bizarre, brusque**) as an experimental technique to test the intelligence of cows!

10. At first His Lordship ignored our respectful greetings, but at length he (**cajoled, vouchsafed**) a brief nod in our direction.

11. For ancient Romans, fleeing from the battlefield was the most (**heinous, immutable**) act of cowardice a soldier could commit.

12. His opinion of his own importance is so grotesquely exaggerated that we have come to regard him as a(n) (**megalomaniac, arbiter**).

13. Although she is well into middle age, my Aunt Sally seems unable to (**vouchsafe, disabuse**) herself of the idea that she is still a teenager.

14. He's so tight with his money that it's just about impossible to (**cajole, transmute**) a nickel out of him, no matter how worthy the cause.

15. The task of education, said the speaker, is to (**trangress, transmute**) the primitive selfishness of the child into socially useful modes of behavior.

16. A(n) (**insurgent, heinous**) group at the convention refused to accept the choices of the regular party leaders.

17. A favorite ploy of the (**arbiter, demagogue**) is to appoint a convenient scapegoat upon whom a misguided populace can vent its anger.

18. His conduct after his mother's death was so (**anomalous, brusque**) that I must conclude he was not in full possession of his faculties.

19. If, as they now claim, they were not aware of the illegal character of their undertaking, why did they plan it so (**cajolingly, surreptitiously**)?

20. In *Gulliver's Travels* and other writings, Jonathan Swift (**vouchsafed, castigated**) the human race for its follies and wickedness.

21. The President complained that government bureaucracy was hobbling his programs with (**fetters, aspersions**) of red tape.

22. What hurt my feelings was not so much his refusal to give me a job as the (**brusque, vicarious**) way in which he told me that he had nothing for me.

Review   Units 4–6

Analogies   *In each of the following, encircle the item that best completes the comparison.*

1. **immutable** is to **change** as
a. insurgent is to raise
b. inscrutable is to erase
c. insular is to tame
d. irrevocable is to recall

2. **pickpocket** is to **filch** as
a. cutthroat is to castigate
b. scofflaw is to flout
c. daredevil is to prognosticate
d. spoilsport is to cajole

3. **unwieldy** is to **handle** as
a. immutable is to quiet
b. salutary is to heal
c. fractious is to control
d. axiomatic is to assume

4. **asymmetrical** is to **balance** as
a. autonomous is to significance
b. anomalous is to function
c. amorphous is to shape
d. axiomatic is to purpose

5. **aggrandize** is to **build up** as
a. retrench is to cut back
b. blazon is to turn over
c. vouchsafe is to put on
d. extricate is to take in

6. **caveat** is to **warn** as
a. addendum is to chide
b. precept is to teach
c. aura is to compliment
d. archetype is to advise

7. **erudite** is to **knowledge** as
a. vapid is to intelligence
b. insular is to sophistication
c. cordial is to talent
d. dexterous is to skill

8. **sneak thief** is to **surreptitious** as
a. schnook is to fractious
b. maven is to scurrilous
c. kvetch is to querulous
d. klutz is to vapid

9. **ennui** is to **bored** as
a. ardor is to excited
b. perplexity is to tired
c. annoyance is to satisfied
d. fatigue is to gleeful

10. **affable** is to **aloof** as
a. fractious is to incorrigible
b. arrogant is to querulous
c. sedulous is to nomadic
d. courteous is to brusque

11. **sleazy** is to **unfavorable** as
a. bizarre is to favorable
b. sedulous is to unfavorable
c. salutary is to favorable
d. gossamer is to unfavorable

12. **produce** is to **farming** as
a. sinecure is to manufacturing
b. contraband is to smuggling
c. gossamer is to mining
d. propensity is to importing

13. **merriment** is to **festive** as
a. worry is to resilient
b. gloom is to sepulchral
c. despair is to equitable
d. fear is to vapid

14. **straitlaced** is to **conventionality** as
a. bizarre is to unconventionality
b. soporific is to conventionality
c. erudite is to unconventionality
d. transient is to conventionality

15. **extricate** is to **embroil** as
a. remonstrate is to expostulate
b. reverberate is to echo
c. repudiate is to avow
d. retrench is to economize

16. **resilient** is to **recoil** as
a. brittle is to bounce
b. pliable is to soar
c. buoyant is to float
d. rigid is to bend

17. **alcohol** is to **soporific** as
a. water is to laxative
b. milk is to pollutant
c. tea is to intoxicant
d. coffee is to stimulant

18. **sleazy** is to **quality** as
a. shoddy is to workmanship
b. heinous is to durability
c. scurrilous is to price
d. scathing is to stylishness

Synonyms　　*In each of the following groups, encircle the word or expression that is most nearly **the same** in meaning as the word in **boldface type** in the introductory phrase.*

1. a **brusque** reply
a. polite　　　b. expected　　　c. curt　　　d. curious

2. a **propensity** to boast
a. aversion　　b. tendency　　c. intention　　d. unwillingness

3. forced to **retrench**
a. explain　　b. economize　　c. leave　　d. resign

4. **amorphous** structures
a. massive　　b. formless　　c. ancient　　d. impressive

5. **sepulchral** tones
a. ghostly　　b. happy　　c. melodious　　d. overpowering

6. an **aura** of respectability
a. atmosphere　　b. result　　c. cause　　d. burden

7. **contrive** to see us
a. scheme　　b. expect　　c. refuse　　d. order

8. accept as **axiomatic**
a. valuable　　b. sacred　　c. worthless　　d. self-evident

9. **transmute** his experiences into fiction
a. force　　b. degrade　　c. transform　　d. collapse

10. a group of **fractious** students
a. stupid　　b. well-dressed　　c. diligent　　d. unruly

11. **filched** a pair of sneakers
a. wore out　　b. bought　　c. stole　　d. cleaned

12. a **resilient** spirit
a. careless　　b. depressed　　c. concerned　　d. buoyant

13. an **anomalous** position
a. usual　　b. abnormal　　c. elevated　　d. high-paying

14. **vouchsafe** a reply
a. expect　　b. grant　　c. deliver　　d. consider

15. **castigate** the students
a. praise　　b. rebuke　　c. amuse　　d. ignore

16. **disabused** her listeners
a. misdirected　　b. confused　　c. praised　　d. set straight

17. **flout** accepted standards
a. observe　　b. disregard　　c. explain　　d. be unaware of

18. seek **vicarious** thrills
a. quiet　　b. safe　　c. substitute　　d. dangerous

19. a ship filled with **contraband**
a. foreigners　　b. illegal imports　　c. liquor　　d. food

20. **straitlaced** standards of behavior
a. lax　　b. vague　　c. stuffy　　d. flexible

R

Shades of Meaning   *Read each sentence carefully. Then encircle the item that best completes the statement below the sentence.*

The fog that morning was so inscrutable that traffic officials were warning drivers not to proceed until it lifted. **(2)**

1. In line 1 the word **inscrutable** most nearly means
  a. incapable of being understood   c. unable to be distinguished
  b. unlikely to cause harm   d. impossible to see through

Smaller and smaller images of the chandeliers and candelabras forever reverberated in the mirrors that encrusted the walls of the great central reception hall. **(2)**

2. The best meaning for the word **reverberated** in line 2 is
  a. thundered   b. were reflected   c. resounded   d. were enlarged

The practice of scourging ordinary seamen severely for even petty offenses lasted well into the 19th century in both the British and the American navies. **(2)**

3. The word **scourging** in line 1 can best be defined as
  a. flogging   b. reprimanding   c. punishing   d. fining

In small-town America one hundred years ago the boardinghouse catered to long-term visitors, while the hotel met the needs of mere transients. **(2)**

4. The best definition of the word **transients** in line 2 is
  a. traveling salespeople   c. people just passing through
  b. tourists on holiday   d. displaced persons

No one who has seen *Cool Hand Luke* will ever forget the shocking scenes of Paul Newman and the other convicts on that Georgia chain gang, fettered together more like animals than human beings. **(2)**

5. In line 3 the word **fettered** can best be defined as
  a. shackled   b. roped   c. tied   d. linked

Antonyms   *In each of the following groups, encircle the word or expression that is most nearly **opposite** in meaning to the word in **boldface type** in the introductory phrase.*

1. repudiate a treaty
a. reject   b. accept   c. publish   d. amend

2. state of **ennui**
a. fatigue   b. depression   c. excitement   d. uncertainty

3. a **soporific** report
a. adequate   b. long-winded   c. disorganized   d. stimulating

4. erudite comments
a. uninformed   b. wordy   c. brief   d. relevant

5. spread **aspersions**
a. praise   b. advice   c. slander   d. rumors

6. a decidedly **insular** viewpoint
a. cosmopolitan   b. bigoted   c. old-fashioned   d. provincial

7. a state of **autonomy**
a. dependence   b. freedom   c. stability   d. financial ruin

8. a **vapid** moving picture
a. foreign   b. dull   c. prize-winning   d. meaningful

9. an **affable** companion
a. talkative   b. unfriendly   c. long-standing   d. faithful

10. an **irrevocable** decision
a. considered   b. hasty   c. minor   d. reversible

11. tried to **aggrandize** her social position
a. clarify   b. diminish   c. improve   d. hide

12. attitudes that **fetter** the mind
a. shackle   b. stultify   c. interest   d. liberate

13. a **sleazy** waterfront hotel
a. colorful   b. classy   c. inexpensive   d. dingy

14. a **heinous** act
a. noble   b. cruel   c. inadvertent   d. wicked

15. a **surreptitious** meeting
a. hasty   b. brief   c. open   d. unexpected

16. **transient** joys
a. selfish   b. permanent   c. passing   d. innocent

17. his **querulous** tone
a. agreeable   b. loud   c. hostile   d. complaining

18. wore a **bizarre** costume
a. colorful   b. ordinary   c. eye-catching   d. strange

19. his **scathing** comments
a. complimentary   b. bitter   c. ungrammatical   d. unjustified

---

Completing the Sentence   *From the following words, choose the one that best completes each of the sentences below. Write the word in the appropriate space.*

Group A

anomalous	cajole	vicarious	extricate
scurrilous	flout	axiomatic	bizarre
sedulous	aggrandize	reverberate	equitable

1. "I must admit that, though far from generous, the settlement is eminently _____ and fairminded," she replied.

2. The harder I struggled to _____ myself from the quicksand, the deeper I seemed to sink into it.

3. I will not permit anyone to either coerce or _____ me into doing something that I know in my heart is wrong.

4. If he applied the same _____ attention to his schoolwork that he does to baseball, he would be an outstanding student.

5. Though she is not displeased with her own accomplishments, she seems to derive a good deal of _____ delight from those of her son.

Group B

unwieldy	**addendum**	**amorphous**	**insurgent**
contraband	**infer**	**precept**	**salutary**
scourge	**brusque**	**sinecure**	**scathing**

1. Of all the _____ that were taught to you by your parents, which one do you consider the most important?

2. What can we _____ from his stubborn refusal to tell us where he was at the time of the crime?

3. The package was so _____ that I had to ask the custodian to help me place it in the car.

4. In the American Revolution, the British forces represented the established government, while the Colonials were the _____ .

5. Far from doing you any harm, a summer spent working on a farm will have a(n) _____ influence, both physically and psychologically.

Word Families

A. *On the line provided, write a **noun form** of each of the following words.*

EXAMPLE: reverberate — **reverberation**

1. affable _____

2. erudite _____

3. inscrutable _____

4. querulous _____

5. remonstrate _____

6. resilient _____

7. scurrilous _____

8. infer _____

9. insular _____

10. cajole _____

B. *On the line provided, write a **verb** related to each of the following words.*

EXAMPLE: contrivance — **contrive**

1. insular _____

2. inference _____

3. transmutation _____

4. aspersion _____

5. cajolery _____

Filling the Blanks   *Encircle the pair of words that best complete the meaning of each of the following passages.*

1. Only the sound of my footsteps _____ through the empty hallway disturbed the _____ silence in which the deserted office building was enveloped. "It's as quiet as a tomb in here at night," I thought as I made my way to the exit.

   a. transgressing . . . gossamer
   b. retrenching . . . anomalous
   c. reverberating . . . sepulchral
   d. transmuting . . . bizarre

2. When I returned from lunch earlier than I had planned, I surprised a little sneak thief _____ attempting to _____ a few dollars from the petty cash drawer.

   a. brusquely . . . retrench
   b. irrevocably . . . vouchsafe
   c. vapidly . . . cajole
   d. surreptitiously . . . filch

3. He is usually so courteous and _____ that I was completely taken aback by his unaccountably _____ and surly reply to my question.

   a. affable . . . brusque
   b. fractious . . . scurrilous
   c. equitable . . . erudite
   d. straitlaced . . . querulous

4. "It took months of _____ effort and astute planning on my part to _____ this company from the mess in which I found it," the new owner smugly boasted. "If I hadn't worked like a dog, the firm would still be in financial hot water."

   a. amorphous . . . cajole
   b. sedulous . . . extricate
   c. immutable . . . contrive
   d. irrevocable . . . disabuse

5. "The American legal system is not _____ , nor are our laws _____ ," the Chief Justice observed. "Like everything else in this fluid world of ours, they change and develop over time."

   a. anomalous . . . autonomous
   b. transient . . . resilient
   c. immutable . . . irrevocable
   d. axiomatic . . . inscrutable

6. Rubber's remarkable _____ to resume its original shape makes it one of the world's most _____ materials.

   a. aura . . . fractious
   b. propensity . . . resilient
   c. autonomy . . . erudite
   d. ennui . . . gossamer

Analogies In each of the following, encircle the letter of the item that best completes the comparison.

1. provincial is to **insular** as
a. occult is to esoteric
b. inadvertent is to deliberate
c. salutary is to baneful
d. fractious is to docile

2. lassitude is to **tired** as
a. sangfroid is to excited
b. resilience is to annoyed
c. ennui is to wearied
d. aplomb is to mortified

3. propensity is to **proclivity** as
a. hiatus is to continuity
b. aura is to atmosphere
c. aspersion is to remark
d. approbation is to disapproval

4. vapid is to **flavor** as
a. sedulous is to industry
b. intrinsic is to value
c. hackneyed is to novelty
d. brusque is to brevity

5. meritorious is to **heinous** as
a. amorphous is to shapeless
b. puzzling is to inscrutable
c. immutable is to permanent
d. bland is to scathing

6. aggrandize is to **bigger** as
a. ascribe is to larger
b. contrive is to smaller
c. ameliorate is to better
d. flout is to shorter

7. intermediary is to **intercede** as
a. interloper is to extricate
b. proponent is to repudiate
c. demagogue is to conciliate
d. arbiter is to adjudicate

8. remonstrate is to **expostulate** as
a. abominate is to vouchsafe
b. castigate is to precipitate
c. wheedle is to cajole
d. ingratiate is to commiserate

9. tenuous is to **strength** as
a. vitriolic is to rancor
b. transient is to permanence
c. equitable is to fairness
d. stringent is to durability

10. querulous is to **fret** as
a. affable is to bellyache
b. petulant is to fuss
c. bizarre is to gripe
d. noncommittal is to complain

Shades of Meaning Read each sentence carefully. Then encircle the item that best completes the statement below the sentence.

On the retreat from Moscow Napoleon's once invincible Grande Armée degenerated into an amorphous mass of frightened fugitives, thanks to the Cossacks and the Russian winter. (2)

1. The word **amorphous,** as used in line 2, most nearly means
a. lacking substance
b. lacking character
c. lacking cohesion
d. lacking limits

"Or like stout Cortez when with eagle eyes
He star'd at the Pacific—and all his men (2)
Looked at each other with a wild surmise—
Silent, upon a peak in Darien." (4)
  (Keats, "On First Looking into Chapman's Homer," 11–14)

2. The word **surmise** in line 3 most nearly means
a. smile of recognition
b. flash of intuition
c. peal of laughter
d. yawn of boredom

"That particular artist is so eclectic," the critic admitted, "that it is impossible to track down absolutely all the tenuous influences on his work." (2)

3. The best meaning for the word **tenuous** in line 2 is
a. unusual   b. vague   c. flimsy   d. various

For certain types of wheel-thrown ceramics a fine, unctuous clay is best; for others a less malleable medium is preferable. (2)

4. The word **unctuous** in line 1 may best be defined as
a. servile   b. dry   c. smug   d. plastic

ICBMs and other types of guided missiles are unfortunately much too fractious to allow for testing anywhere near populated areas, however thinly inhabited. (2)

5. The best definition for the word **fractious** in line 1 is
a. unpredictable b. dangerous   c. quarrelsome d. expensive

Filling the Blanks   *Encircle the pair of words that best complete the meaning of each of the following sentences.*

1. If the job you have is nothing more than a(n) _____ , you don't have to be a particularly _____ or talented worker to handle it.
a. hiatus . . . erudite
b. prerogative . . . noncommittal
c. sinecure . . . sedulous
d. archetype . . . soporific

2. The flames from the blazing tire factory bathed the whole neighborhood in a(n) _____ , unearthly glow, and the acrid stench of burning rubber _____ the midnight air.
a. vapid . . . transmuted
b. lurid . . . permeated
c. sleazy . . . transcended
d. amorphous . . . simulated

3. The sonorous notes of the mighty organ _____ through the _____ vaults and cavernous expanses of the cathedral like the distant roar of thunder.
a. reverberated . . . sepulchral
b. blazoned . . . unctuous
c. expostulated . . . surreptitious
d. retrenched . . . circuitous

4. In many ancient religions, the _____ of an entire community would periodically be placed on the head of a single sacrificial animal, so that the death of one might _____ the sins of all.
a. innuendoes . . . fetter
b. surmises . . . enjoin
c. aspersions . . . expedite
d. transgressions . . . expiate

5. Though _____ have passed since the day Moses brought them down from the top of Mt. Sinai, the _____ of justice and righteousness contained in the Ten Commandments are still revered by peoples of many faiths throughout the world.
a. epitomes . . . caveats
b. millennia . . . precepts
c. addenda . . . coalitions
d. umbrages . . . archetypes

Unit 7

Definitions *From the words in Group A and Group B following, choose the one that most nearly corresponds to each definition below. Write the word on the line at the right of each definition and in the illustrative phrase below it.*

Group A

austere (ô 'stēr)
beneficent (bə 'nef ə sənt)
cadaverous (kə 'dav ər əs)
concoct (kän 'käkt)
crass (kras)
debase (di 'bās)

desecrate ('des ə krāt)
desist (di 'zist)
disconcert (dis kən 'sərt)
grandiose ('gran dē ōs)
inconsequential
(in kän sə 'kwen shəl)

1. (*v.*) to commit sacrilege, treat irreverently; to contaminate, pollute   _____

_____ the cemetery

2. (*adj.*) trifling, unimportant   _____

ignore the _____ details

3. (*v.*) to prepare by combining ingredients, make up (as a dish); to devise, invent, fabricate   _____

_____ a new vegetable stew

4. (*v.*) to confuse; to disturb the composure of   _____

_____ him with an unexpected question

5. (*adj.*) pale, gaunt, resembling a corpse   _____

their _____ appearance

6. (*adj.*) grand in an impressive or stately way; marked by pompous affectation or grandeur, absurdly exaggerated   _____

a victim of her own _____ ideas

7. (*v.*) to lower in character, quality, or value; to degrade, adulterate; to cause to deteriorate   _____

_____ the nation's currency

8. (*adj.*) performing acts of kindness or charity; conferring benefits, doing good   _____

a(n) _____ deity

9. (*adj.*) coarse, unfeeling; stupid   _____

_____ indifference to our problems

10. (*v.*) to cease doing something, forbear   _____

ask them to _____ immediately

11. (*adj.*) severe or stern in manner; without adornment or luxury, simple, plain; harsh or sour in flavor   _____

the _____ conduct of the Puritans

58

Group B

infraction (in 'frak shən)
mitigate ('mit ə gāt)
pillage ('pil ij)
prate (prāt)
punctilious (pəŋk 'til ē əs)
redoubtable (ri 'daü tə bəl)

reprove (ri 'prüv)
restitution (res tə 'tü shən)
stalwart ('stôl wərt)
stipend ('stī pend)
vulnerable ('vəl nər ə bəl)

12. (*n.*) a breaking of a law or obligation _____
    paid the penalty for his _____

13. (*adj.*) inspiring fear or awe; illustrious, eminent _____
    trembling as he faced the _____ warrior

14. (*v.*) to rob of goods by open force (as in war),
    plunder; (*n.*) the act of looting; booty _____
    _____ the town mercilessly

15. (*adj.*) open to attack; capable of being wounded
    or damaged; unprotected _____
    found themselves in a(n) _____ position

16. (*n.*) a fixed sum of money paid periodically for
    services or to defray expenses _____
    pay her assistants an adequate _____

17. (*v.*) to talk a great deal in a foolish or aimless
    fashion _____
    _____ endlessly about their deeds

18. (*n.*) the act of restoring someone/something to the
    rightful owner or to a former state or position;
    making good for loss or damage _____
    _____ for the damage to the car

19. (*adj.*) very careful and exact, attentive to fine
    points of etiquette or propriety _____
    _____ in observing the rules

20. (*adj.*) strong and sturdy; brave; resolute; (*n.*) a
    brave, strong person; a strong supporter; one who
    takes an uncompromising position _____
    the _____ pioneers

21. (*v.*) to find fault with, scold, rebuke _____
    _____ their children for their unruly conduct

22. (*v.*) to make milder or softer, to moderate in force
    or intensity _____
    _____ her anger by offering an apology

**Completing
the Sentence**

*From the words for this unit, choose the one that best
completes each of the following sentences. Write the
word in the space provided.*

1. They _____ the funeral service by talking loudly during the
ceremonies, laughing, and generally showing a complete lack of respect.

2. An official who is responsible for shaping vital national policies should not
waste time and energy on such _____ matters.

3. His work on behalf of the homeless was merely the latest in a long line of
_____ undertakings.

4. Before they arrived home from the party, they _____ an
elaborate story that they hoped would excuse their being two hours late.

5. Our democracy, I believe, is more _____ to decay from
within than it is to attack from the outside.

6. Though most of our players were the equals of theirs, the awesome size of
their _____ center filled us with apprehension.

7. At a time when we need a modest, low-cost housing program, how can
we be expected to accept such a(n) _____ scheme?

8. I'm telling you this is not to _____ you for having made a
mistake but to prevent the mistake from being repeated.

9. Fond remembrances of happy days of family life intensified rather than
_____ her grief.

10. Unless we can persuade them to _____ from their plans to
tear down the goalposts after the game, there may be serious disorder.

11. Is there any way that we can make _____ for the terrible
wrong we have done them?

12. I became desperately tired of listening to him _____ about
how important he was, how much money he had, and so forth.

13. Who can ever forget those pictures showing the _____
faces of the people who had been in concentration camps!

14. I found that beneath Mr. Peccarero's rather _____ manner
and appearance there was a warm, sympathetic person.

15. Though she looked rather frail, her _____ spirit made her a
tireless crusader for women's rights.

16. She has _____ her considerable talents by writing books
which are designed to appeal to the lowest tastes.

17. In addition to paying my tuition fees, the scholarship allows me a monthly
_____ for living expenses.

18. It is hard to forgive the _____ selfishness with which they took most of the food supplies for their own use.

19. We are, I trust, long past the time when it was considered quite "natural" for newly elected officials to _____ the city treasury.

20. Even a so-called minor _____ of the traffic laws may lead to a serious accident.

21. Whenever she serves as chairperson, she is so _____ that she insists on observing every fine point of parliamentary procedure.

22. He went right on with his speech, refusing to be _____ by the heckling of a few loudmouths.

Synonyms   From the words for this unit, choose the one that is most nearly **the same** in meaning as each of the following groups of expressions. Write the word on the line given.

1. compensation, reimbursement, redress; restoration _____

2. sturdy, stout; intrepid, valiant; a mainstay _____

3. formidable, fearsome, awesome; august _____

4. to chatter, prattle, blab, babble, palaver _____

5. precise, scrupulous, exacting; fussy, finicky _____

6. defenseless, exposed, unguarded _____

7. to ravage, sack, loot; booty _____

8. to cheapen, corrupt, demean, depreciate _____

9. trivial, negligible, petty, trifling _____

10. to upset, rattle, ruffle, faze, perturb _____

11. to lessen, relieve, alleviate, diminish _____

12. to create, fashion, fabricate; to rustle up _____

13. corpselike, wasted, haggard, emaciated, ghastly _____

14. to chide, chastise, upbraid, reproach _____

15. forbidding, rigorous; puritanical, ascetic; unadorned, subdued _____

16. a salary, wage, allowance, emolument _____

17. humanitarian, magnanimous, charitable _____

18. majestic; bombastic, highfalutin _____

19. to profane, defile, violate _____

20. crude, vulgar, tasteless, oafish; obtuse _____

21. a violation, transgression, breach, offense _____

22. to stop, discontinue, refrain, suspend _____

Antonyms From the words for this unit, choose the one that is most nearly **opposite** in meaning to each of the following groups of expressions. Write the word on the line given.

1. selfish, cruel; harmful, deleterious _____

2. careless, negligent, lax, perfunctory _____

3. robust, portly; rosy, the picture of health _____

4. to aggravate, intensify, irritate, exacerbate _____

5. to elevate, uplift, improve, enhance _____

6. to continue, proceed, prolong, resume _____

7. invincible, protected, safe, secure _____

8. to revere, honor, venerate, consecrate _____

9. weak, infirm; irresolute, vacillating _____

10. refined, elegant, tasteful, polished; brilliant _____

11. simple, modest, unaffected, humble _____

12. to praise, commend, laud, pat on the back _____

13. important, essential, crucial, vital _____

14. mild, indulgent; luxurious; flamboyant _____

15. to relax, calm, put at ease _____

16. to come to the point, not waste words _____

17. laughable, risible, contemptible _____

Choosing the Right Word Encircle the **boldface** word that more satisfactorily completes each of the following sentences.

1. The conductor of the orchestra was so (**desecrated, disconcerted**) by the noisy audience that he stopped the performance and asked for quiet.

2. In her clumsy efforts to be recognized as an "intellectual," she (**prates, desecrates**) endlessly about matters she does not really understand.

3. His (**grandiose, beneficent**) schemes for world conquest collapsed in a nightmare of military defeat and internal revolt.

4. She is such a(n) (**redoubtable, crass**) foe of the trite phrase that her students tremble lest her wrath descend on them for using a cliché.

5. As (**restitution, infraction**) for the damage he had caused to the family car, Phil promised to clean and polish it regularly for a full year.

6. Her self-confidence is so overweening that she is simply not (**grandiose, vulnerable**) to "put-down" remarks that would annoy other people.

7. It is a (**desecration, restitution**) of the memory of Lincoln to involve his name in defense of such a racist policy.

8. The master chef has (**debased, concocted**) a dessert that is so rich that it will be a menace to weight watchers throughout the country.

9. The woman is known and loved throughout the community for her many (**redoubtable, beneficent**) acts in behalf of all types of unfortunates.

10. Although his conduct may not have violated any law, I consider it a gross (**cadaver, infraction**) of conventional ethical standards.

11. He is so (**punctilious, austere**) about every detail of dress that it is said he presses his shoelaces before wearing them.

12. That sum may seem (**inconsequential, vulnerable**) to you, but to me it is a great deal of money.

13. The starving children shown in the TV special looked more like (**cadavers, stalwarts**) than living creatures.

14. The law cannot regulate the way people feel about the rights of minority groups, but it *can* force people to (**desist, reprove**) from activities that would infringe on those rights.

15. The professor agreed to the modest (**infraction, stipend**) offered for the position provided that the college supply her with the free use of a house.

16. The principal (**disconcerted, reproved**) the entire student body for their discourteous behavior toward the guest speaker at the school assembly.

17. Since my next paycheck was not to be had until the first of the month, I reconciled myself to living (**austerely, inconsequentially**) until then.

18. The fact that he did everything possible to help the poor child after the accident tends to (**mitigate, desecrate**) his responsibility for the tragedy.

19. The sale of so many great works of art to foreign collectors is, in my eyes, little more than (**pillage, mitigation**) of our cultural heritage.

20. By concentrating on personal gain, he has (**debased, disconcerted**) both himself and the high office to which he was elected.

21. Whenever I go to a concert, I seem to spend half my time shushing the (**crass, austere**) boors who chitchat while the orchestra is playing.

22. All the power of Great Britain could not shake the American colonists in their (**stalwart, beneficent**) opposition to measures that they considered unfair and tyrannical.

Unit 8

Definitions   *From the words in Group A and Group B following, choose the one that most nearly corresponds to each definition below. Write the word on the line at the right of each definition and in the illustrative phrase below it.*

Group A

acrimonious (ak rə 'mō nē əs)
bovine ('bō vīn)
conducive (kən 'dü siv)
consternation (kän stər 'nā shən)
corpulent ('kôr pyə lənt)
disavow (dis ə 'vaů)

dispassionate (dis 'pash ə nət)
dissension (di 'sen shən)
dissipate ('dis ə pāt)
élan (ā 'län)
expurgate ('ek spər gāt)

1. (*n.*) an enthusiastic vigor and liveliness, spirit; a flair _____

    act the part of Cyrano with _____

2. (*v.*) to cause to disappear; to scatter, dispel; to spend foolishly, squander; to be extravagant in pursuit of pleasure _____

    _____ her energies on trivia

3. (*v.*) to deny responsibility for or connection with _____

    _____ any part in the plot

4. (*adj.*) tending to promote or assist, helpful, favorable _____

    an atmosphere _____ to learning

5. (*v.*) to remove objectionable passages or words from a written text; to cleanse, purify _____

    _____ the article

6. (*adj.*) impartial; calm, free from emotion _____

    a(n) _____ view of the matter

7. (*n.*) dismay, confusion _____

    viewed the mess with _____

8. (*n.*) disagreement, sharp difference of opinion _____

    creating _____ in the membership

9. (*adj.*) resembling a cow or ox; sluggish, unresponsive _____

    a(n) _____ personality

10. (*adj.*) stinging, bitter in temper or tone _____

    shocked me with her _____ reply

11. (*adj.*) fat; having a large, bulky body _____

    grown _____ with the years

Group B

gauntlet ('gônt lət)	**perfidy** ('pər fə dē)
hypothetical (hī pə 'thet ə kəl)	**relegate** ('rel ə gāt)
ignoble (ig 'nō bəl)	**squeamish** ('skwē mish)
impugn (im 'pyün)	**subservient** (səb 'sər vē ənt)
intemperate (in 'tem pər ət)	**susceptible** (sə 'sep tə bəl)
odium ('ō dē əm)	

12. (*adj.*) subordinate in capacity or role; serving to promote some end; submissively obedient _____

completely _____ to her commands

13. (*n.*) faithlessness, treachery _____

a base act of _____

14. (*adj.*) based on an assumption or guess; used as a provisional or tentative idea to guide or direct investigation _____

a(n) _____ situation

15. (*v.*) to call into question; attack as false _____

_____ my honesty

16. (*n.*) hatred, contempt; disgrace or infamy resulting from hateful conduct _____

heap _____ on the tyrant

17. (*adj.*) immoderate, lacking in self-control; inclement _____

his _____ outbursts of anger

18. (*adj.*) mean, low, base _____

led astray by _____ motives

19. (*adj.*) inclined to nausea; easily shocked or upset; excessively fastidious or refined _____

a(n) _____ person

20. (*adj.*) open to; easily influenced; lacking in resistance _____

one who is _____ to colds

21. (*n.*) an armored or protective glove; a challenge to combat; two lines of men armed with weapons with which to beat a person forced to run between them; an ordeal _____

a knight's _____

22. (*v.*) to place in a lower position; to assign, refer, turn over; to banish _____

_____ to a mere clerical job

Completing the Sentence — *From the words for this unit, choose the one that best completes each of the following sentences. Write the word in the space given.*

1. I am not trying to _____ his truthfulness, but I still do not see how the facts support his claims.

2. Under the American form of government, all branches of the military are clearly _____ to the civilian authority.

3. Because Vidkun Quisling betrayed his country, Norway, to the Nazis, his name has become a symbol of _____ .

4. People with a tendency toward being _____ must wage a lifelong struggle against rich foods.

5. Our discussion that day was a(n) _____ one, based on the possibility—still far from definite—that I would take the job.

6. Last-minute cramming for examinations is scarcely _____ to earning high grades.

7. Thomas Bowdler _____ Shakespeare's plays because he felt that they were unfit to "be read aloud in a family."

8. The figure-skating champion performed with such _____ that the other competitors seemed tame and lifeless in comparison.

9. To the _____ of the people in the stands, the lion leaped out of the cage and bounded toward the exit.

10. Though her overall position seemed to be sensible, her language was so tactless and _____ that people wouldn't support her.

11. Anyone as _____ as Pete will have trouble accustoming himself to the sights, sounds, and smells of hospital work.

12. She is a person of such fine moral standards that she seems incapable of a(n) _____ act.

13. Now that these ugly facts about his business dealings have come to light, I must _____ my support of his candidacy.

14. The job of cleaning up the field and the stands after the big game was _____ to the freshmen.

15. We have had enough of high-powered, excited oratory; what we need now is a(n) _____ examination of the facts.

16. He is so _____ to flattery that with a few complimentary words I can get him to do almost anything I want.

17. Far from presenting a unified front, the party is torn by all kinds of strife and _____ .

18. The bold candidate threw down the _____ and dared her opponent to face her in a televised debate.

19. Vigorous debate is fine, but is there any real need for such outlandishly strident and _____ name-calling?

20. Instead of using all their forces in one concerted attack on the enemy, they _____ their strength in minor engagements.

21. The _____ for this tragic failure does not belong to any individual or small group but to the community as a whole.

22. Although she seems rather plodding in her behavior and rarely becomes excited, I think it is unfair to call her "_____."

Synonyms *From the words for this unit, choose the one that is most nearly **the same** in meaning as each of the following groups of expressions. Write the word on the line given.*

1. to disown, disclaim, retract, abjure _____

2. to transfer, consign; to demote, banish _____

3. secondary; useful; servile, obsequious _____

4. to challenge, deny, dispute, query, question _____

5. a dare, provocation; a trial, punishment _____

6. vulnerable to, receptive; impressionable _____

7. to purge, censor, bowdlerize _____

8. betrayal, disloyalty, treason, duplicity _____

9. assumed, supposed, conjectural, conditional _____

10. abhorrence, opprobrium, shame, ignominy _____

11. unbiased, disinterested, cool, detached _____

12. inferior, unworthy, dishonorable, sordid _____

13. to disperse, strew, diffuse; to waste _____

14. nauseous, queasy; delicate, oversensitive; priggish _____

15. verve, dash, zest, panache, brio _____

16. shock, amazement, bewilderment _____

17. strife, discord, contention _____

18. beneficial, contributive, fostering _____

19. biting, caustic, rancorous, hostile, peevish _____

20. overweight, heavy, obese, stout, portly _____

21. stolid, dull, slow, stupid _____

22. excessive, extreme, unrestrained, inordinate _____

Antonyms *From the words for this unit, choose the one that is most nearly **opposite** in meaning to each of the following groups of expressions. Write the word on the line given.*

1. gentle, warm, mild, friendly, cordial _____

2. moderate, restrained, cool and collected _____

3. to acknowledge, admit, grant, certify _____

4. esteem, admiration, approbation _____

5. faithfulness, loyalty, steadfastness _____

6. admirable, praiseworthy, lofty, noble _____

7. to gather, collect; to conserve, husband _____

8. slender, lean, spare, gaunt, emaciated _____

9. actual, real, tested, substantiated _____

10. lifelessness, listlessness, enervation _____

11. resistant, immune _____

12. primary, principal; bossy, domineering _____

13. unhelpful, unfavorable, hindering, blocking _____

14. committed, engaged; partial, biased _____

15. agreement, accord, harmony _____

16. alert, sharp, bright, keen, quick _____

Choosing the Right Word *Encircle the **boldface** word that more satisfactorily completes each of the following sentences.*

1. The retiring coach said he no longer had the stomach to run the (**gauntlet, odium**) of critics who assailed him after every loss.

2. It is not for me to (**expurgate, impugn**) his motives, but how could anyone except an overambitious scoundrel have misled his friends in that way?

3. I am not ordinarily a (**corpulent, squeamish**) person, but the sight of that terrible automobile accident haunted me for weeks.

4. My Spanish friend Pablo Rivera finds it hard to understand the (**odium, dissension**) attached to bullfighting in most non-Hispanic countries.

5. I noticed with some distaste how her usually overbearing manner became (**susceptible, subservient**) when our employer joined the group.

6. Though I was annoyed by the child's behavior, the father's outburst of anger seemed to me deplorably (**intemperate, bovine**).

7. A certain amount of disagreement is healthy in any organization, but in our club (**dissension, perfidy**) has become almost a way of life.

8. Try your best to subdue your natural reluctance and make a (**squeamish, dispassionate**) decision that will be in your son's best interests.

9. A policy that is beneficial to some individuals and groups may not be (**conducive, acrimonious**) to the economic health of the entire nation.

10. Aren't you going a little far when you accuse me of (**consternation, perfidy**) because I didn't vote for you in the beauty contest?

11. By reference to (**hypothetical, ignoble**) cases, you may be able to clarify the difference between "murder" and "manslaughter" for the law students.

12. Not too long ago in our society, a (**corpulent, bovine**) body was generally admired as a sign of prosperity and physical vigor.

13. Imagine our (**consternation, dissension**) when the brakes failed and we headed full speed toward the busy intersection!

14. Students who have been well trained in the social sciences should not be (**susceptible, ignoble**) to the cheap fallacies of racism.

15. It is not the quality of her voice, which is only average, but the (**perfidy, élan**) with which she performs that makes her such a favorite.

16. There is often a thin line between the kind of debate that is spirited and useful and that which is (**acrimonious, conducive**) and nonproductive.

17. The estate he had inherited from his father was (**dissipated, disavowed**) in a long series of impractical and/or mismanaged business enterprises.

18. Their (**susceptible, bovine**) stares and obvious inability to understand the seriousness of the situation made me doubt their mental capacity.

19. Far from being (**ignoble, dispassionate**), her failure after making a valiant effort may serve as an inspiration to young people.

20. If we are going to be required to perform a(n) (**expurgated, relegated**) version of the play, then I think it is not worth doing.

21. When Mr. Kummer saw my pathetically inept efforts to prepare a banana split, I was (**impugned, relegated**) to the ranks of the unemployed.

22. The prisoner attempted to (**disavow, dissipate**) his confession on the grounds that he had not been informed of his legal rights.

Unit 9

Definitions *From the words in Group A and Group B following, choose the one that most nearly corresponds to each definition below. Write the word on the line at the right of each definition and in the illustrative phrase below it.*

Group A

abate (ə ′bāt)
adulation (aj ə ′lā shən)
anathema (ə ′nath ə mə)
astute (ə ′stüt)
avarice (′av ər is)
culpable (′kəl pə bəl)

dilatory (′dil ə tôr ē)
egregious (i ′grē jəs)
equivocate (i ′kwiv ə kāt)
evanescent (ev ə ′nes ənt)
irresolute (ir ′ez ə lüt)

1. (*n.*) praise or flattery that is excessive   _____

enjoyed the _____ of the fans

2. (*adj.*) vanishing, soon passing away; light and airy   _____

the _____ charm of youth

3. (*adj.*) not on time, not prompt; tending to delay   _____

_____ in paying bills

4. (*v.*) to make less in amount, degree, etc.; to subside, become less; to nullify; to deduct, omit   _____

wait until the storm _____

5. (*adj.*) unable to make up one's mind, hesitating   _____

be _____ in a time of danger

6. (*adj.*) shrewd, crafty, showing practical wisdom   _____

_____ management of money

7. (*n.*) a greedy desire, particularly for wealth   _____

the miser's ever-growing _____

8. (*adj.*) conspicuous, standing out from the mass (used particularly in an unfavorable sense)   _____

guilty of a(n) _____ blunder

9. (*adj.*) deserving blame, worthy of condemnation   _____

_____ neglect of their duties

10. (*n.*) an object of intense dislike; a curse or strong denunciation (often used adjectivally without the article)   _____

declare racial prejudice to be _____

11. (*v.*) to speak or act in a way that allows of more than one interpretation; to be deliberately vague or ambiguous   _____

an annoying tendency to _____

70

Group B

modicum ('mäd ə kəm)
nebulous ('neb yə ləs)
novice ('näv is)
penury ('pen yə rē)
pretentious (prē 'ten shəs)
recapitulate (rē kə 'pich ə lāt)

resuscitate (ri 'səs ə tāt)
slovenly ('sləv ən lē)
succinct (sək 'siŋkt)
supposition (səp ə 'zish ən)
torpid ('tôr pid)

12. (adj.) untidy, dirty, careless

shocked by their _____ attire

13. (n.) something that is assumed or taken for granted without conclusive evidence

a fact, not a mere _____

14. (adj.) expressed briefly and clearly; (clothing) lacking in fullness of cut

issue a(n) _____ statement

15. (v.) to review a series of facts; to sum up

pause to _____ the main points

16. (adj.) cloudlike, resembling a cloud; cloudy in color, not transparent; vague, confused, indistinct

confused by their _____ account of the accident

17. (v.) to revive, bring back to consciousness or existence

_____ the rescued swimmer

18. (adj.) inactive, sluggish, dull

in a(n) _____ state after the long, dull lecture

19. (n.) one who is just a beginner at some activity requiring skill and experience (also used adjectivally)

mistakes typical of a(n) _____

20. (n.) extreme poverty; barrenness, insufficiency

the _____ of their circumstances

21. (n.) a small or moderate amount

try to get by with a(n) _____ of effort

22. (adj.) done for show, striving to make a big impression; claiming merit or position unjustifiably; making demands on one's skill or abilities, ambitious

a(n) _____ remark

Completing the Sentence   *From the words for this unit, choose the one that best completes each of the following sentences. Write the word in the space given.*

1. After giving us extremely detailed instructions for more than an hour, she _____ briefly and then sent us out on our assignments.

2. As he gave a(n) _____ account of what had happened, we admired his ability to reduce a complicated matter to its essentials.

3. If you had shown just a(n) _____ of patience, you would not have become involved in such a fix.

4. I was impressed by the _____ way our hostess guided the conversation away from topics that might be embarrassing to her guests.

5. It will mean more to him to gain the approval of the few people who can appreciate his work than to receive the _____ of the crowd.

6. Your brilliant plan is based on one false _____ —that I am willing to work without pay.

7. Tom was so _____ about whether to go out for basketball or swimming that he ended by going out for neither.

8. Isn't it strange that a young person who spends hours making sure that he or she looks "just right" for a big date is often so _____ at other times?

9. Her mind, _____ as a result of hours of exposure to the bitter cold, was not alert enough to sense the impending danger.

10. Since I truly loathe people who think they are "above the common herd," any form of snobbery is absolutely _____ to me.

11. Using the most modern and up-to-date equipment, the firefighters worked tirelessly to _____ the victim of smoke inhalation.

12. Since Tony was a(n) _____ at bridge, the three veteran players hoped to find someone more suitable to fill out their table.

13. The _____ she had experienced in her childhood and youth made her keenly aware of the value of money.

14. As her anger slowly _____ , she realized that such childish outbursts of emotion would do nothing to help solve her problems.

15. I don't think I'd call such a(n) _____ grammatical mistake a minor "slip of the pen."

16. How can you consider him _____ when the accident was caused by a landslide that no one could have foreseen or prevented?

17. Sure, it's great to be a big-league ballplayer but bear in mind that the years of stardom are brief and _____ .

18. The study of history teaches us that a hunger for land, like other kinds of

_____ , is the cause of a great many wars.

19. He holds forth in great detail on what is wrong with our city government,

but the remedies he suggests are exceedingly _____ .

20. Although she tried to _____ , we insisted on a simple "yes" or "no" answer.

21. Does he use all those quotations as a means of clarifying his meaning, or

simply as a(n) _____ display of his learning?

22. When you are _____ in returning a book to the library, you are preventing someone else from using it.

Synonyms   *From the words for this unit, choose the one that is most nearly* **the same** *in meaning as each of the following groups of expressions. Write the word on the line given.*

1. an iota, jot, speck, bit, dollop   _____

2. sluggish, lethargic, otiose, languid   _____

3. hazy, fuzzy, cloudy, vague, murky, opaque; indeterminate   _____

4. an assumption, presumption, hypothesis   _____

5. to revive, revitalize, restore   _____

6. indecisive, vacillating, wavering   _____

7. concise, terse, compact, pithy   _____

8. ephemeral, transient, transitory   _____

9. a beginner, neophyte, tyro   _____

10. tardy, laggard, procrastinating   _____

11. to review, summarize, sum up, go over   _____

12. a malediction, imprecation; an abomination   _____

13. delinquent, peccant; blameworthy   _____

14. destitution, want, indigence   _____

15. glaring, flagrant, blatant   _____

16. adoration, idolization, hero-worship   _____

17. inflated, ostentatious, affected   _____

18. to diminish, decrease; to subside, let up   _____

19. shrewd, acute; sagacious, judicious; wily   _____

20. to talk out of both sides of one's mouth _____

21. greed, cupidity, rapacity, acquisitiveness _____

22. unkempt, slatternly; slipshod, lax _____

Antonyms   *From the words for this unit, choose the one that is most nearly **opposite** in meaning to each of the following groups of expressions. Write the word on the line given.*

1. a benediction, blessing _____

2. tidy, neat, well-groomed, natty, dapper _____

3. definite, distinct, clear, sharply focused _____

4. a veteran, past master, pro, expert _____

5. obtuse, doltish, empty-headed, dumb _____

6. unassuming, unaffected, modest _____

7. a deluge, avalanche; an excess, surplus _____

8. ridicule, derision, scorn, odium _____

9. blameless, innocent; laudable, meritorious _____

10. prompt, punctual; speedy, expeditious _____

11. to intensify, increase, magnify, wax _____

12. everlasting, immortal, imperishable _____

13. determined, decisive, unwavering _____

14. affluence, abundance, luxury, opulence _____

15. wordy, prolix, verbose, garrulous _____

16. energetic, dynamic, vigorous _____

17. to speak one's mind plainly _____

18. unnoticeable, paltry, piddling _____

Choosing the   *Encircle the **boldface** word that more satisfactorily*
Right Word   *completes each of the following sentences.*

1. Biologists have a theory that every plant or animal in the course of its development (**abates, recapitulates**) all the stages of its evolution.

2. The heat in the room, the quiet drone of the fly at the window, and the bright sunlight put me into a (**torpid, slovenly**) state.

3. Only a (**modicum, novice**) at golf would have tried to use a driver when hitting into such a strong wind.

4. The reporter gave the rewrite man a (**nebulous, succinct**) account of what had happened, and he expanded it into a feature story.

5. They say that school spirit at Central High is dead, but I am confident that it can be (**resuscitated, equivocated**) if the right methods are used.

6. As a result of (**irresolution, egregiousness**) when that novel was first submitted, the publishing house lost the biggest best-seller of the year.

7. If there were just a (**penury, modicum**) of decency in his makeup, he would be a far better person than he is now.

8. When the results of her mistakes became public knowledge, she gained a well-deserved reputation for being an (**astute, egregious**) blunderer.

9. He is completely indifferent to wealth and luxurious living; his (**anathema, avarice**) is directed instead toward fame and prestige.

10. In playing chess, she deliberately uses (**dilatory, nebulous**) tactics to make her opponent impatient and tense.

11. Since he is known to be a multimillionaire, it seems almost (**culpable, pretentious**) of him, in an inverted sense, to drive around in a small, battered, inexpensive car.

12. Sportswriters attribute the success of the pennant-winning team largely to the (**astute, evanescent**) managing of old Buck Coakley.

13. What do you think of the concept that when a crime is committed, society is often as (**culpable, astute**) as the criminal?

14. We rightly (**anathematize, recapitulate**) all forms of racism, but we should feel sympathy, rather than hatred, for the individual racist.

15. In everyone's life, a situation may arise that calls for a basic moral choice to be made, without compromise or (**abatement, equivocation**).

16. What she calls her "philosophy of life" seems to me a hodgepodge of childish fallacies and (**nebulous, dilatory**) generalizations.

17. As soon as the hurricane (**abated, equivocated**), rescue teams rushed out to help people in the devastated area.

18. In the densely populated and underdeveloped countries we visited, we saw the depths to which people can be reduced by (**penury, anathema**).

19. The glory of this perfect spring day seems to be all the more precious because it is so (**torpid, evanescent**).

20. The (**slovenly, pretentious**) physical appearance of the report was matched by its careless writing and disorganized content.

21. You may be right in your belief that Jan won't let us use her car, but remember that this is still only a(n) (**anathema, supposition**).

22. Is it any wonder that a 17-year-old star athlete reacts so erratically when she receives such (**recapitulation, adulation**) from the entire school?

Analogies   *In each of the following, encircle the item that best completes the comparison.*

1. **aggravate** is to **mitigate** as
a. repudiate is to disavow
b. pillage is to betray
c. intensify is to abate
d. reprove is to falsify

2. **irresolute** is to **determination** as
a. ignoble is to simplicity
b. inconsequential is to patience
c. dispassionate is to fairness
d. intemperate is to moderation

3. **egregious** is to **mountain** as
a. punctilious is to pigsty
b. grandiose is to foxhole
c. dispassionate is to toadstool
d. inconsequential is to molehill

4. **expurgate** is to **censor** as
a. impugn is to lie
b. pillage is to plunder
c. desecrate is to cheat
d. dissipate is to steal

5. **avarice** is to **grasping** as
a. humility is to bare-knuckled
b. perfidy is to tight-fisted
c. acrimony is to light-fingered
d. generosity is to open-handed

6. **idol** is to **adulation** as
a. anathema is to odium
b. crony is to acrimony
c. novice is to supposition
d. scholar is to consternation

7. **crass** is to **refinement** as
a. squeamish is to conscience
b. punctilious is to etiquette
c. ignoble is to honor
d. stalwart is to decisiveness

8. **gauntlet** is to **hand** as
a. visor is to leg
b. helmet is to head
c. javelin is to arm
d. shield is to foot

9. **susceptible** is to **immunity** as
a. vulnerable is to protection
b. conducive is to exemption
c. culpable is to infraction
d. acrimonious is to dissension

10. **palace** is to **grandiose** as
a. mansion is to austere
b. shack is to pretentious
c. hovel is to penurious
d. cottage is to slovenly

11. **laggard** is to **dilatory** as
a. novice is to inexperienced
b. cadaver is to lively
c. coward is to grandiose
d. bully is to torpid

12. **nebulous** is to **clarity** as
a. egregious is to significance
b. torpid is to energy
c. succinct is to brevity
d. hypothetical is to relevance

13. **starvation** is to **cadaverous** as
a. dieting is to corpulent
b. gluttony is to obese
c. austerity is to plump
d. revelry is to squeamish

14. **dapper** is to **slovenly** as
a. shrewd is to astute
b. punctilious is to scrupulous
c. modest is to pretentious
d. benificent is to urbane

15. **redoubtable** is to **awe** as
a. piteous is to compassion
b. evanescent is to adulation
c. squeamish is to misgiving
d. dispassionate is to enthusiasm

16. **traitor** is to **perfidy** as
a. dunce is to élan
b. novice is to penury
c. judge is to restitution
d. miser is to avarice

17. **consternation** is to **disconcert** as
a. adulation is to disavow
b. aspersion is to impugn
c. astonishment is to dumfound
d. élan is to debase

18. **bovine** is to **sluggish** as
a. horsey is to squeamish
b. canine is to corpulent
c. feline is to crass
d. swinish is to slovenly

Identification *In each of the following groups, encircle the word that is best defined or suggested by the introductory phrase.*

1. living in acute want
a. penury   b. pillage   c. odium   d. adulation

2. "I can't stand the sight of blood!"
a. dilatory   b. evanescent   c. squeamish   d. bovine

3. under the authority of others
a. stalwart   b. benificent   c. irresolute   d. subservient

4. a fixed payment for services rendered
a. anathema   b. stipend   c. avarice   d. infraction

5. someone who has just learned to play bridge
a. novice   b. consternation   c. corpulent   d. hypothetical

6. provide some comfort for our deep sorrow
a. debase   b. intemperate   c. mitigate   d. equivocate

7. testimony that is unemotional and unprejudiced
a. crass   b. dispassionate   c. succinct   d. culpable

8. revive a plan that has been abandoned
a. resuscitate   b. prate   c. disconcert   d. disavow

9. "I do not believe that his motives are as unselfish as he pretends."
a. concoct   b. torpid   c. modicum   d. impugn

10. demoted me to the second team
a. desist   b. relegate   c. desecrate   d. abate

11. a tennis player who we know is too good for any of us
a. austere   b. punctilious   c. grandiose   d. redoubtable

12. regained her citizenship by act of Congress
a. dissension   b. restitution   c. perfidy   d. supposition

13. behavior that is dishonest, selfish, and cowardly
a. inconsequential   b. vulnerable   c. ignoble   d. pretentious

14. "Now, let's review the main points, one by one."
a. recapitulate   b. nebulous   c. reprove   d. conducive

Shades of Meaning *Read each sentence carefully. Then encircle the item that best completes the statement below the sentence.*

Not surprisingly, the tyrant's much-touted troop of stalwarts, once on the battlefield, proved utter cravens, turning and fleeing at the mere sound of gunfire. (2)

1. In line 1 the word **stalwarts** most nearly means
a. gallants   b. supporters   c. loyalists   d. bullies

The grapes from that region produce a full-bodied wine with a decidedly austere flavor—quite the opposite of the smooth, fruity, but somewhat watery vintages characteristic of other parts of the country. (2)

2. The word **austere** in line 2 is used to mean
a. solemn   b. plain   c. subdued   d. harsh

R

Among their many gods the ancient Egyptians were particularly attached to the bovine Hathor, the goddess of love and mirth and the personification of the sky. (2)

3. The best meaning for the word **bovine** in line 2 is
a. represented as a cow
c. sluggish and unresponsive
b. zoomorphic
d. dim-witted

"Aurora's rosy fingers gently stroke the sky
And dissipate the inky vestiges of Night." (2)
　　(A.E. Glug, "Prating in the Prater," 77–78)

4. The word **dissipate** in line 2 may best be defined as
a. squander　　b. carouse　　c. dispel　　d. waste

A teaspoonful of "Roach-Rout" powder, mixed with a quart of water, produces a nebulous, strong-smelling liquid that is highly toxic to cockroaches and other household pests but perfectly safe for pets. (2)

5. The best meaning for the word **nebulous** in line 2 is
a. fuzzy　　b. cloudy　　c. vague　　d. confused

Antonyms　　*In each of the following groups, encircle the word or expression that is most nearly **opposite** in meaning to the word in **boldface type** in the introductory phrase.*

1. torpid behavior
a. cordial　　b. quiet　　c. talkative　　d. energetic

2. led to **consternation**
a. self-assurance　b. fear　　c. boredom　　d. disorganization

3. ordered them to **desist**
a. relax　　b. cease　　c. begin　　d. speak

4. grandiose plans
a. modest　　b. intricate　　c. unselfish　　d. far-ranging

5. led **austere** lives
a. obscure　　b. self-indulgent　c. simple　　d. wholesome

6. an **inconsequential** action
a. foolish　　b. significant　　c. clever　　d. minor

7. adulation of the public
a. protection　　b. admiration　　c. hostility　　d. patronage

8. a **pretentious** personality
a. proud　　b. self-respecting　c. self-effacing　d. unpleasant

9. dissension in the ranks
a. fighting　　b. discussion　　c. discipline　　d. agreement

10. when the storm **abates**
a. passes　　b. intensifies　　c. ends　　d. occurs

11. to **debase** oneself
a. elevate　　b. examine　　c. criticize　　d. dress

12. disconcert the speaker
a. reassure　　b. ignore　　c. mortify　　d. announce

13. with an **egregious** lack of judgment
a. laughable   b. conspicuous   c. unnoticeable   d. unpredictable

14. **culpable** behavior
a. meritorious   b. criminal   c. bizarre   d. deliberate

15. **disavow** their support
a. accept   b. reject   c. pay for   d. be ashamed of

16. their **slovenly** appearance
a. conspicuous   b. well-groomed   c. unattractive   d. vulgar

17. made a **succinct** statement
a. offensive   b. forceful   c. long-winded   d. surprising

18. the **stalwart** hallway guards
a. uniformed   b. delicate   c. armed   d. redoubtable

19. his **intemperate** criticism
a. restrained   b. bitter   c. eloquent   d. irrational

20. such **beneficent** actions
a. humanitarian   b. harmful   c. well-planned   d. constructive

---

Completing the Sentence   *From the following words, choose the one that best completes each of the sentences below. Write the word in the appropriate space.*

Group A

corpulent	acrimonious	egregious	astute
hypothetical	slovenly	élan	stalwart
vulnerable	pillage	infraction	bovine

1. I don't agree that the offenders should be penalized severely for so slight a(n) _____ of the rules.

2. The investments he had made were so _____ that they gave his widow a good income for the rest of her life.

3. "Their exchange on the House floor wasn't particularly friendly," I observed, "but it wasn't particularly _____ , either."

4. The mission of our armed forces is to liberate the conquered territories— not to _____ them.

5. Let us consider a(n) _____ case—a typical young married couple with two dependents and an income of $35,000 a year.

Group B

expurgate	supposition	nebulous	concoct
odium	perfidy	cadaverous	reprove
avarice	crass	desecrate	punctilious

1. We can excuse an honest mistake, however harmful, but we will never forgive an act of deliberate _____ .

2. Rosalind is so _____ about her reports that if a page is even slightly marked up, she will retype it entirely.

3. Because he was chosen to enforce those extremely unpopular laws, he became the object of public _____ .

4. I don't know if I have ever in my life witnessed an instance of such _____ stupidity!

5. What need is there to _____ the text of a book that has been read and enjoyed by young people for generations?

Word Families

A. *On the line provided, write a **noun form** of each of the following words.*
EXAMPLE: grandiose — **grandiosity**

1. abate _____

2. astute _____

3. culpable _____

4. austere _____

5. evanescent _____

6. irresolute _____

7. pretentious _____

8. recapitulate _____

9. resuscitate _____

10. succinct _____

B. *On the line provided, write a **verb** related to each of the following words.*
EXAMPLE: dissipation — **dissipate**

1. pretentious _____

2. dissension _____

3. anathema _____

4. evanescent _____

5. supposition _____

6. conducive _____

7. adulation _____

8. restitution _____

9. hypothetical _____

10. dilatory _____

**Filling
the Blanks**

*Encircle the pair of words that best complete the
meaning of each of the following passages.*

1. In A.D. 267, a band of barbarous Heruli raided the ancient Greek religious
   center at Delphi. For several days they _____ the town and
   _____ its temples. Then they rode off, laden with booty.

   a. relegated . . . dissipated
   b. resuscitated . . . debased
   c. pillaged . . . desecrated
   d. disconcerted . . . expurgated

2. "Those who circumvent the law are often as _____ as those
   who actually break it," the lawyer remarked. "The seriousness of such an
   offense is rarely _____ by the fact that, technically, no crime
   has been committed."

   a. culpable . . . mitigated
   b. crass . . . abated
   c. vulnerable . . . impugned
   d. susceptible . . . disavowed

3. For a minor _____ of the rules of a hockey game, the
   offending player is _____ to the penalty box, or "sin bin,"
   for two minutes. For a more serious violation, he is put there for five.

   a. anathema . . . recapitulated
   b. infraction . . . relegated
   c. supposition . . . disavowed
   d. dissension . . . debased

4. Though a few lucky "haves" are able to provide themselves with all the
   comforts of life on a truly _____ scale, the bulk of the
   people in many third-world countries seem to live like paupers in the
   most extreme state of _____ and neglect.

   a. egregious . . . avarice
   b. crass . . . dissension
   c. redoubtable . . . perfidy
   d. grandiose . . . penury

5. A person has to have a strong stomach to work in a funeral parlor or
   morgue. Handling _____ is definitely not a job for the
   _____ .

   a. modicums . . . slovenly
   b. novices . . . redoubtable
   c. cadavers . . . squeamish
   d. concoctions . . . acrimonious

6. The _____ of history forever attaches itself to the name of
   Benedict Arnold for his villainous act of _____ during the
   American Revolution.

   a. acrimony . . . beneficence
   b. odium . . . perfidy
   c. consternation . . . equivocation
   d. anathema . . . restitution

Analogies   *In each of the following, encircle the item that best completes the comparison.*

1. marauder is to **pillage** as
a. insurgent is to expostulate
b. embezzler is to peculate
c. archetype is to desecrate
d. critic is to repudiate

2. assuage is to **mitigate** as
a. reverberate is to enjoin
b. flout is to filch
c. concoct is to contrive
d. transgress is to relegate

3. crass is to **grossness** as
a. dilatory is to speediness
b. succinct is to firmness
c. vapid is to dullness
d. tenuous is to forcefulness

4. sangfroid is to **consternation** as
a. umbrage is to resentment
b. avarice is to penury
c. aplomb is to clumsiness
d. ferment is to turmoil

5. supposition is to **hypothetical** as
a. equivocation is to nebulous
b. innuendo is to scathing
c. addendum is to inscrutable
d. precept is to circuitous

6. debase is to **worse** as
a. permeate is to better
b. simulate is to worse
c. ameliorate is to better
d. prognosticate is to worse

7. novice is to **callow** as
a. slob is to slovenly
b. crony is to acrimonious
c. brigand is to unctuous
d. arbiter is to brusque

8. evanescent is to **transient** as
a. unwieldy is to manageable
b. austere is to opulent
c. immutable is to invariable
d. stalwart is to irresolute

9. astute is to **acumen** as
a. dispassionate is to foresight
b. fractious is to wisdom
c. ignoble is to skill
d. erudite is to learning

10. punctilious is to **details** as
a. insular is to possessions
b. intrinsic is to values
c. straitlaced is to morals
d. meritorious is to awards

Shades of Meaning   *Read each sentence carefully. Then encircle the item that best completes the statement below the sentence.*

The views and values typically inculcated by the gang mindset usually precipitate themselves in various concrete behavior patterns, some of which are decidedly antisocial.   **(2)**

1. The best meaning for the word **precipitate** in line 2 is
a. embody   b. hurry   c. provoke   d. rain

For years the feelings and experiences of Proust's youth fermented in his brain before they distilled out in one of the world's greatest works, *A la récherche du temps perdu.*   **(2)**

2. The word **fermented** in line 1 most nearly means
a. lay dormant   b. cluttered   c. jostled about   d. brewed

As we stood chatting around the water cooler yesterday, our supervisor inferred, much to everyone's dismay, that our usual holiday bonuses would not be forthcoming this year.   **(2)**

3. In line 2 the word **inferred** may best be defined as
a. stated   b. surmised   c. implied   d. gathered

"Or is it that some Force, too wise, too strong,
Even for yourselves to conquer or beguile,   (2)
Sweeps earth and heaven, and men, and gods along
Like the broad volume of the insurgent Nile?"   (4)
    (Mathew Arnold, "Mycerinus," 37–40)

4. The best meaning for the word **insurgent** in line 4 is
   a. muddy   b. rushing   c. rebellious   d. salty

"Americans are proud of the great waterways of our nation," the senator
said, "and don't wish to see them desecrated by industrial waste and   (2)
other contaminants."

5. The word **desecrated** in line 2 is best defined as
   a. profaned   b. exhausted   c. polluted   d. misused

Filling the Blanks   *Encircle the pair of words that best complete the meaning of each of the following sentences.*

1. Like a summer thundershower, whose violence quickly _____ and is forgotten, his fits of temper were intense but _____ .
   a. retrenches . . . tenuous   c. resuscitates . . . brusque
   b. abates . . . transient   d. dissipates . . . immutable

2. Since no salary or _____ of any kind was attached to the job, election to the Roman consulship eventually became the special _____ of a small group of wealthy nobles, who could afford the privilege of serving their country for a year without pay.
   a. restitution . . . sinecure   c. amnesty . . . proclivity
   b. contraband . . . epitome   d. stipend . . . prerogative

3. Attila the Hun soon came to be called "the _____ of God" because the terror and devastation he wrought were looked upon as divine retribution for the _____ of a wayward and recalcitrant Roman people.
   a. Scourge . . . transgressions   c. Fetter . . . infringements
   b. Aura . . . infractions   d. Hiatus . . . exhortations

4. Since all forms of idolatry were _____ to the Old Testament prophets, they _____ relentlessly against such abhorrent practices and castigated the people who persisted in adhering to them.
   a. heinous . . . expurgated   c. anathema . . . inveighed
   b. salutary . . . expostulated   d. axiomatic . . . remonstrated

5. To the rather _____ and squeamish Victorians, some of Shakespeare's language was so objectionable that they would only read his plays in _____ versions like those produced by Thomas Bowdler.
   a. jaded . . . ameliorated   c. erudite . . . disabused
   b. straitlaced . . . expurgated   d. crass . . . expedited

Unit 10

Definitions   *From the words in Group A and Group B following, choose the one that most nearly corresponds to each definition below. Write the word on the line at the right of the definition and in the illustrative phrase below it.*

Group A

accrue (ə 'krü)
annotation (an ə 'tā shən)
antediluvian (an tē də 'lü vē ən)
bedlam ('bed ləm)
covert ('kō vərt)
debonair (deb ə 'nâr)

dun (dən)
efficacious (ef ə 'kā shəs)
equanimity (ek wə 'nim ə tē)
fortuitous (fôr 'tü ə təs)
gist (jist)

1. (*adj.*) accidental, happening by chance   _____

_____ comings and goings

2. (*adj.*) hidden, disguised, purposefully kept secret; sheltered, secluded; (*n.*) a sheltered place, a hiding place   _____

_____ operations

3. (*n.*) a state or scene of uproar and confusion   _____

virtual _____ on the convention floor

4. (*adj.*) pleasant, courteous, lighthearted; smooth and polished (in manners and appearance)   _____

a(n) _____ young gentleman

5. (*n.*) a critical or explanatory note or comment, especially for a literary work   _____

provide _____ for the plays of Shakespeare

6. (*n.*) the essential part, main point, or essence   _____

repeat the _____ of my comments

7. (*adj.*) effective, producing results   _____

a(n) _____ program to improve our community

8. (*v.*) to grow or accumulate in the course of time; to happen as a natural result   _____

allowed the interest to _____ for many years

9. (*v.*) to demand insistently, especially payment of a debt; (*n.*) a creditor; (*adj.*) dark, dull, drab, dingy, blackish   _____

_____ their debtors

10. (*n.*) calmness, composure, refusal to panic   _____

bear misfortune with _____

11. (*adj.*) relating to or typical of ancient times; antiquated   _____

a(n) _____ steamboat

Group B

gratuitous (grə 'tü ə təs)
imperious (im 'pir ē əs)
inimical (in 'im ə kəl)
invective (in 'vek tiv)
motley ('mät lē)
munificent (myü 'nif ə sənt)

procrastinate (prə 'kras tə nāt)
provocative (prə 'väk ə tiv)
recondite ('rek ən dīt)
reprobate ('rep rə bāt)
sedentary ('sed ən ter ē)

12. (*adj.*) tending to produce a strong feeling or response; arousing desire or appetite; irritating, annoying; (*n.*) something that provokes or stimulates _____

deliberately _____ behavior

13. (*adj.*) characterized by or calling for continued sitting; remaining in one place _____

a(n) _____ job

14. (*adj.*) overbearing, arrogant; seeking to dominate; pressing, compelling _____

resented her _____ manner

15. (*adj.*) freely given; not called for by circumstances, unwarranted _____

surprised by his _____ insults

16. (*v.*) to delay, put off until later _____

_____ so long that the opportunity was lost

17. (*adj.*) exceeding ordinary knowledge and understanding, profound, abstruse _____

immersed in _____ studies

18. (*adj.*) extremely generous, lavish _____

a(n) _____ gift

19. (*adj.*) unfriendly, hostile; harmful, unfavorable _____

_____ to our best interests

20. (*adj.*) showing great diversity or variety; composed of different elements or many colors; (*n.*) a multicolored woolen fabric; a jester's costume; a jester; a mixture of odd elements _____

the _____ costume of the circus clown

21. (*n.*) a strong denunciation or condemnation; abusive language; (*adj.*) abusive, vituperative _____

stunned by the unexpected _____

22. (*n.*) a depraved, vicious, or unprincipled person, scoundrel; (*adj.*) wicked, corrupt, or unprincipled; (*v.*) to disapprove of, condemn _____

an unregenerate old _____

Completing
the Sentence

From the words for this unit, choose the one that best completes each of the following sentences. Write the word in the space given.

1. Next day, the instructor returned my theme with a number of comments, queries, and other _____ penciled in the margin.

2. The revolutionary forces were a(n) _____ group, made up of people of all ages, backgrounds, and political sympathies.

3. Anyone who _____ when the opportunity to make a very profitable deal presents itself is not going to be notably successful in the business world.

4. His elegant appearance was matched by the _____ ease and polish of his manners.

5. She is a leader who can command loyalty and instant obedience without resorting to abusive language, threats, or a(n) _____ manner.

6. Daily exercise is recommended particularly for people whose occupations are for the most part _____ .

7. It will be helpful if you can state the _____ of his arguments in a few sentences.

8. Although she said nothing to indicate her true feelings, the expression on her face gave away her _____ sympathy for the young culprits.

9. If you resent being _____ by tradespeople, why not try paying your bills on time?

10. In view of the fact that I have been driving for many years without having a single accident, his advice on how to handle a car seemed entirely _____ .

11. _____ broke out in the meeting hall as the speaker tried vainly to be heard over the angry shouting of the audience.

12. The basic theory of the United States Constitution is that concentration of power in any one branch of the government is _____ to freedom.

13. Think of the great advantages that will _____ to all of us if we can carry out a truly effective program to conserve and maintain our natural resources.

14. Their methods of running the family business are not just out-of-date; they are positively _____ .

15. Our meeting seemed at the time to be entirely _____ , but I learned later that it was the result of a careful plan.

16. This research program is entirely devoted to developing a drug that will be _____ in the treatment of arthritis.

17. The editorial on "Legal Rights for Teenagers" was so _____ that it brought in more letters to the editor than any other single article we published all year.

18. The kinds of books I enjoy reading range from light and airy comedies to _____ studies of social and philosophical problems.

19. No sooner had the incorrigible old _____ gotten out of jail than he returned to the wicked ways that had landed him there in the first place.

20. My opponent's last speech was filled with such wild charges, acrimonious language, and bitter _____ that I walked out of the room without even trying to reply.

21. The _____ gift of the Mellon family made it possible to set up the National Gallery of Art in Washington, D.C.

22. We have seen her accept victory with grace; now can she face defeat with _____ ?

23. It is up to the courts to decide how far police authorities may go in making use of _____ means of surveillance to catch criminals.

24. Although their language was deliberately _____ , I did not allow it to cause me to lose my self-control.

25. As the British writer W. S. Maugham once observed, human nature is a(n) _____ collection of strengths and weaknesses, foibles and fortes.

Synonyms   *From the words for this unit, choose the one that is most nearly **the same** in meaning as each of the following groups of expressions. Write the word on the line given.*

1. stimulating, arousing; vexing, galling; a stimulus, incentive   _____

2. vituperation, abuse; a diatribe, philippic   _____

3. variegated; heterogeneous, diverse; a fool   _____

4. the substance, essence, core, nucleus   _____

5. seated, sitting; stationary, static   _____

6. immoral, corrupt; a scoundrel, blackguard   _____

7. composure, tranquillity, imperturbability   _____

8. bounteous, generous, lavish, liberal   _____

9. to stall, temporize, delay, dillydally _____

10. to hound, pester, harass, nag _____

11. effective, effectual; potent, powerful _____

12. antagonistic; deleterious, pernicious _____

13. commotion, pandemonium; chaos, anarchy _____

14. domineering, overbearing, magisterial; urgent, imperative _____

15. superannuated, archaic, antiquated _____

16. abstruse, esoteric, arcane _____

17. undercover, clandestine, sub-rosa _____

18. a critical or explanatory footnote _____

19. unjustified, uncalled-for, unwarranted; voluntary _____

20. gracious, suave, urbane; carefree _____

21. accidental, unintentional, chance, random _____

22. to accumulate; to result, proceed from _____

Antonyms   From the words for this unit, choose the one that is most nearly **opposite** in meaning to each of the following groups of expressions. Write the word on the line given.

1. intentional, deliberate, premeditated _____

2. simple, easy to understand, uncomplicated _____

3. justified, warranted _____

4. friendly, favorable; beneficial, salutary _____

5. active; peripatetic, migratory, vagrant _____

6. a tribute, panegyric, encomium _____

7. uniform, homogeneous, monochromatic _____

8. fawning, obsequious; humble, unassuming _____

9. boorish, churlish; distraught, agitated _____

10. stingy, miserly, tightfisted, parsimonious _____

11. peace and quiet, order, tranquillity _____

12. modern, up-to-date, state-of-the-art _____

13. open, overt, undisguised   _____

14. upright, virtuous, moral; a saint   _____

15. excitability, flappability, agitation   _____

16. ineffective; worthless, useless   _____

17. dull, insipid, bland, unstimulating   _____

18. to strike while the iron is hot   _____

19. to dwindle, decrease, diminish, lessen   _____

20. bright, gaudy, flashy   _____

Choosing the Right Word   *Encircle the **boldface** word that more satisfactorily completes each of the following sentences.*

1. Scientists believe that everything in nature occurs in accordance with invariable laws and that nothing is truly (**imperious, fortuitous**).

2. Instead of relying on facts and logic, she used all kinds of rhetorical tricks and slashing (**invective, equanimity**) to attack her opponent.

3. His tone of voice was so (**munificent, imperious**) that I wasn't sure if he was asking me for a loan or demanding payment of tribute.

4. During the war, soldiers assigned to desk jobs were sometimes called sarcastically the "chairbound infantry" or the "(**sedentary, recondite**) commandos."

5. The old proverb "Make haste slowly" is an endorsement of prudence—not of (**invective, procrastination**).

6. Instead of that highly involved and (**recondite, debonair**) discussion of the nation's energy needs, why don't you tell us simply what we can do to help solve the problem?

7. It is generally agreed that we urgently need more (**efficacious, reprobate**) methods of handling criminals, both for their own benefit and for that of the public.

8. Although they claimed that their summary gave us the (**bedlam, gist**) of the resolution, the fact is that it omitted important details.

9. My sad story is that after working for three hours in the hot sun cleaning up the yard, I received the (**imperious, munificent**) sum of $1.75.

10. What good will it do you to (**dun, procrastinate**) me so mercilessly when you know that I am flat broke?

11. To bear evils with (**invective, equanimity**) doesn't mean that you should make no effort to correct them.

12. Jeremy thinks of himself as a combination of the good looks of Robert Redford, the wit of John Cleese, and the (**debonair, inimical**) charm of Paul Newman.

13. "The crass and (**reprobate, fortuitous**) conduct on the part of those who were responsible for the scandal certainly deserved all the condemnation public opinion and the news media accorded it," I observed.

14. Only a genius could have converted such a (**motley, gratuitous**) group of individuals, drawn from all walks of life, into a disciplined and efficient organization.

15. The scholars who compiled the notes and (**annotations, provocations**) for my portable edition of Chaucer did a superb job of clarifying obscure or puzzling words and passages.

16. We shall oppose any changes in the labor code that appear (**inimical, efficacious**) to the health and safety of workers.

17. I wouldn't refer to her record collection as (**"antediluvian," "fortuitous"**) because it contains a few disks made as long as five years ago.

18. Things were already hectic in our tiny apartment, but when my sister arrived with two very excited dogs, the place was thrown into absolute (**bedlam, annotation**).

19. Since you've never seen me play tennis, your assumption that you can beat me is quite (**imperious, gratuitous**).

20. I am convinced that some substantial advantages will surely (**accrue, procrastinate**) to me if I complete my college education.

21. He tried to make it appear that he was speaking in a friendly spirit, but I detected the (**inimical, covert**) malice beneath the "harmless" remarks.

22. This new book is a(n) (**imperious, provocative**) examination of our school system that may upset some of your most cherished ideas about higher education.

23. We appreciated the services he furnished (**gratuitously, inimically**), but we soon came to see that it would have been cheaper to pay for a really professional job.

24. In the mental picture I have of old Mr. Benz, he is in a (**sedentary, covert**) position, half asleep, before his TV set.

25. Instead of withdrawing the interest payments, why don't you let them (**procrastinate, accrue**) in your savings account?

Unit 11

Definitions   *From the words in Group A and Group B following, choose the one that most nearly corresponds to each definition below. Write the word on the line at the right of the definition and in the illustrative phrase below it.*

Group A

abstemious (ab 'stē mē əs)
accentuate (ak 'sen chü āt)
censurable ('sen shər ə bəl)
contingent (kən 'tin jənt)
corroborate (ke 'räb ə rāt)
denizen ('den ə zən)

discursive (dis 'kər siv)
disseminate (di 'sem ə nāt)
dowdy ('dau dē)
florid ('flär id)
foist (foist)

1. (*n.*) an inhabitant, resident; one who frequents a place   _____

    the scaly _____ of our rivers and lakes

2. (*adj.*) likely but not certain to happen, possible; dependent on uncertain events or conditions; happening by chance;
(*n.*) a representative group forming part of a larger body   _____

    _____ on my parents' approval

3. (*v.*) to impose by fraud; to pass off as worthy or genuine; to bring in by stealth, dishonesty, or coercion   _____

    _____ such rubbish on the public

4. (*v.*) to confirm, make more certain   _____

    a witness to _____ my statements

5. (*adj.*) moderate, sparing (as in eating and drinking); characterized by abstinence and self-discipline   _____

    frugal and _____ in their habits

6. (*v.*) to scatter widely   _____

    in order to _____ her views

7. (*adj.*) highly colored, reddish; excessively ornate, overdecorated, showy   _____

    a(n) _____ style of architecture

8. (*adj.*) deserving of blame or correction   _____

    a(n) _____ act

9. (*adj.*) passing aimlessly from one place or subject to another, rambling, roving, nomadic   _____

    a(n) _____ account of his life

10. (*adj.*) poorly dressed, shabby; lacking smartness and good taste

_____

her _____ appearance

11. (*v.*) to emphasize, place stress on

_____

makeup that _____ a person's natural beauty

Group B

gauche (gōsh)
heresy ('her ə sē)
inculcate ('in kəl kāt)
palpable ('pal pə bəl)
perceptive (pər 'sep tiv)
pernicious (pər 'nish əs)

quail (kwāl)
salient ('sāl yənt)
satiate (*v.*, 'sā shē āt; *adj.*, 'sā shē it)
sear (sir)
specious ('spē shəs)

12. (*adj.*) deceptive, apparently good or valid but lacking real merit

_____

a(n) _____ claim on our support

13. (*adj.*) having sympathetic insight or understanding, capable of keen appreciation

_____

have a(n) _____ eye for values

14. (*adj.*) capable of being touched or felt; easily seen, heard, or recognized

_____

a(n) _____ absurdity

15. (*v.*) to make or become dry and withered; to char or scorch the surface of; to harden or make unfeeling

_____

plants _____ by the burning sun and hot, dry winds of summer

16. (*v.*) to satisfy completely; to fill to excess; (*adj.*) full, satisfied

_____

_____ with too much moviegoing

17. (*adj.*) awkward, lacking in social graces, tactless, clumsy

_____

a(n) _____ remark

18. (*v.*) to impress on the mind by repetition, teach persistently and earnestly

_____

_____ good work habits in young students

19. (*n.*) an opinion different from accepted belief; the denial of an idea that is generally held sacred

_____

be accused of _____

20. (*adj.*) extremely harmful; deadly, fatal   _____

      a(n) _____ influence on young people

21. (*v.*) to shrink back in fear, lose heart in a difficult
or dangerous situation   _____

      _____ at the thought of being discovered

22. (*adj.*) leaping, jumping, or springing forth;
prominent, standing out, conspicuous; (*n.*) a
projection or bulge, a land form that projects
upward or outward   _____

      the _____ feature of the new plan

**Completing
the Sentence**

*From the words for this unit, choose the one that best
completes each of the following sentences. Write the
word in the space given.*

1. If I had the time, I could point out many flaws in the _____
arguments you find so impressive.

2. It is hard to believe that people coming from such a refined social milieu

could be so _____ and boorish in their behavior.

3. After the long summer vacation, I was _____ with loafing
and eager to return to school!

4. Her _____ remarks gave us a new and much more realistic
insight into the problem.

5. Since we wished our group to have some say in the town council's final

decision, we sent a small _____ of our most articulate and
convincing speakers to the hearings.

6. Psychologists tell us that the years of early childhood are the best time to

_____ basic concepts of right and wrong.

7. When I referred to her favorite singer as an "untalented, overpaid, and
conceited lout," she looked at me in shock, as though I had been guilty

of _____ .

8. Is there any need for me to describe at length the _____
effects of bad companions on impressionable young people?

9. No honest mechanic will try to _____ inferior replacement
parts on his customers.

10. His talk on world affairs was so disorganized and _____
that it left us more confused than ever.

11. Though this may not be the smartest-looking blouse I own, I thought to

myself, it certainly doesn't make me look _____ !

12. By wearing those bright, light-colored, and tightly fitting clothes, you simply _____ the fact that you are many pounds overweight.

13. The purpose of this program is to _____ throughout the community information about job-training opportunities for young people.

14. When I see the awesome body armor of the redoubtable knights of old, I can easily understand why some of their opponents _____ in fear before them.

15. I don't like to criticize your behavior, but I feel obliged to tell you that your discourtesy to that confused tourist was highly _____ .

16. Unless you can produce witnesses to _____ your claim that you stopped at the red light, the mere assertion will have little or no effect on the jury.

17. Among all those pale and sallow people, her highly _____ complexion stood out like a beacon.

18. The old fellow did indeed look like a typical _____ of the racetrack, as described in Damon Runyon's famous stories.

19. If you wish to seal in the juices and bring out the flavor of your pot roast, _____ it briefly in a hot pan before you put it in the oven.

20. Her good health in old age is due in large part to the _____ habits of her younger years.

21. The stubborn refusal to give me a chance to compete for the scholarship on the same basis as everyone else is a(n) _____ injustice to the whole idea of fair play.

22. A(n) _____ characteristic of every great athlete is the ability to perform at maximum efficiency when under extreme pressure.

23. My participation in that skiing junket to Aspen next month is unfortunately _____ upon getting the necessary time off from the office.

24. We can't ignore the negative elements in life, but it's a good idea always to try to _____ the positive.

Synonyms *From the words for this unit, choose the one that is **the same** in meaning as each of the following groups of expressions. Write the word on the line given.*

1. clumsy, tactless, uncouth, maladroit   _____

2. injurious, deleterious, baleful, noxious   _____

3. deceptively plausible, sophistic, casuistic   _____

4. digressive, diffuse, rambling, episodic   _____

5. an unorthodox belief; heterodoxy _____

6. to instill, implant, infuse, ingrain, imbue _____

7. to pass off, palm off, fob off _____

8. to parch, desiccate; to singe, brown _____

9. to gratify; to cloy, surfeit, gorge _____

10. conspicuous, prominent; protrusive _____

11. conditional, dependent; a detachment _____

12. tangible; plain, obvious, manifest _____

13. a resident, inhabitant; an habitué _____

14. to spread far and wide, broadcast, blazon _____

15. insightful, discerning, observant _____

16. to shrink, recoil, cower, flinch _____

17. to accent, stress, emphasize _____

18. flushed, ruddy; flowery, frilly, ornate _____

19. sparing, moderate, temperate _____

20. blameworthy, discreditable, reprehensible _____

21. to bolster, substantiate, verify _____

22. frumpy, tacky, frowzy, drab _____

Antonyms From the words for this unit, choose the one that is most nearly **opposite** in meaning to each of the following groups of expressions. Write the word on the line given.

1. to downplay, de-emphasize, soft-pedal _____

2. chic, stylish, smart, fashionable _____

3. orthodoxy _____

4. inconspicuous; recessive _____

5. harmless, innocuous; salutary, salubrious _____

6. to efface, extirpate, root out _____

7. pale, ashen, pallid, sallow; austere, stark _____

8. short and to the point, succinct _____

9. to refute, contradict, undermine, discredit _____

10. indulgent, immoderate, intemperate _____

11. an alien, outsider, stranger, foreigner _____

12. adroit, tactful, diplomatic, politic _____

13. dense, thick, obtuse, dimwitted _____

14. valid, sound, solid, genuine _____

15. intangible, insubstantial, incorporeal _____

16. to bring together, concentrate, muster;
to conceal, hide _____

17. commendable, laudable, meritorious _____

18. to stand firm _____

19. independent of, unconnected with; certain _____

20. to starve, deprive entirely of _____

Choosing the Right Word   *Encircle the **boldface** word that more satisfactorily completes each of the following sentences.*

1. Her (**perceptive, florid**) writing style, abounding in adjectives and fancy metaphors, is far from suitable for factual newspaper stories.

2. In a series of (**searing, contingent**) attacks now known as the *Philippics,* Cicero launched his entire battery of political invective against the hapless Mark Antony.

3. We are most likely to fall victim to (**discursive, specious**) reasoning when we have an emotional desire to believe what we are being told.

4. Some English queens were strikingly elegant and imposing figures; others were somewhat (**florid, dowdy**) and unprepossessing.

5. Let's not allow them to (**foist, accentuate**) on us ideas and programs that have been proved failures in other countries!

6. The idea that we can solve our problem by borrowing money to meet the payments on our debts is (**palpably, perceptively**) absurd.

7. Perhaps he did not originate that vicious rumor, but he certainly shares the responsibility for having (**seared, disseminated**) it.

8. Children are often remarkably (**discursive, perceptive**) in understanding how adults feel about them.

9. Out of all the endless flow of dull verbiage in that long lecture, we could recognize only two or three (**gauche, salient**) points.

10. The leaden sky of that bleak November day only served to (**accentuate, inculcate**) the gloom I felt at the sudden death of my best friend.

11. I (**quailed, seared**) so much at the prospect of undergoing major surgery that my hands literally trembled as I entered the hospital.

12. The most tragic aspect of a forest fire is its destructive effects on the innumerable plant and animal (**denizens, heresies**) of that environment.

13. Although the essays are highly (**discursive, dowdy**), covering a wide range of topics, they are written with such clarity and grace that they are easy to follow.

14. No doubt his efforts to advance his own interests were (**censurable, florid**), but let's try to keep a sense of proportion and not condemn him too much.

15. She was so (**palpable, abstemious**) that she extended her self-control even to her beloved music, and listened to records no more than an hour each day.

16. All the available evidence (**corroborates, foists**) my theory that the theft was planned by someone familiar with the layout of the house.

17. As the Scottish poet Robert Burns aptly suggests, even the best laid plans are often entirely (**palpable, contingent**) on events over which we have no earthly control.

18. The study of history teaches us that many ideas regarded as (**heresies, disseminations**) by one generation are accepted as sound and orthodox by the next.

19. Before we start out to (**inculcate, foist**) certain principles in our young people, let's be very sure that these principles are truly desirable for them and their society.

20. He thought he was being witty and charming, but I regard his conduct at the party as altogether (**abstemious, gauche**).

21. The more we studied the drug problem, the more we became aware of its (**florid, pernicious**) influence on the American people today.

22. I rather like the better TV game shows, but I find that after a certain point, I'm (**satiated, foisted**) and ready for more substantial fare.

23. Modern nutritionists emphasize that there is a(n) (**palpable, abstemious**) difference between "eating to live" and "living to eat."

24. Although the Declaration of Independence was framed only to justify a revolution in the British colonies in North America, its ideas and ideals have been (**disseminated, accentuated**) throughout the world.

25. Her (**florid, pernicious**) personality was in sharp contrast to the quiet, restrained demeanor of her younger sister.

26. The silence in their home when we made the condolence call was so (**perceptive, palpable**) that we could almost reach out and touch it.

Unit   12

Definitions   *From the words in Group A and Group B following, choose the one that most nearly corresponds to each definition below. Write the word on the line at the right of the definition and in the illustrative phrase below it.*

Group A

absolve (ab 'zälv)
caricature ('kar i kə chür)
clangor ('klang ər)
contiguous (kən 'tig yü əs)
cupidity (kyü 'pid ə tē)
deleterious (del ə 'tir ē əs)

enhance (en 'hans)
enthrall (en 'thrôl)
extenuate (ek 'sten yü āt)
exude (ek 'süd)
implicit (im 'plis it)

1. (*n.*) a loud ringing sound; (*v.*) to make a loud ringing noise   _____

the _____ of the alarm bell

2. (*adj.*) harmful, injurious   _____

a(n) _____ effect

3. (*v.*) to clear from blame, responsibility, or guilt   _____

_____ them of responsibility for the tragedy

4. (*v.*) to raise to a higher degree; to increase the value or desirability of   _____

planted shrubs to _____ the beauty of the grounds

5. (*n.*) a representation (especially a drawing) in which the subject's characteristic features are deliberately exaggerated; (*v.*) to present someone or something in a deliberately distorted way   _____

an amusing _____ of the President

6. (*v.*) to lessen the seriousness or magnitude of an offense by making partial excuses   _____

circumstances that tend to _____ the crime

7. (*adj.*) side by side, touching; near; adjacent in time   _____

the lot _____ to the one my father owns

8. (*v.*) to ooze out; to discharge through the pores; to emanate (as a quality or a personal impression)   _____

to _____ confidence

9. (*adj.*) implied or understood though unexpressed; without doubts or reservations, unquestioning; potentially contained in   _____

a(n) _____ assumption

10. (*n.*) an eager desire for something; greed   _____

an unhappy victim of his own _____

11. (v.) to enslave; to imprison; to captivate, charm, hold spellbound

_____

_____ us with her masterful performance

Group B

incisive (in 'sī siv)
ostentatious (äs ten 'tā shəs)
paragon ('par ə gän)
paraphrase ('par ə frāz)
politic ('päl ə tik)
preeminent (prē 'em ə nənt)

prosaic (prō 'zā ik)
redundant (ri 'dən dənt)
sanctimonious (saŋk tə 'mō nē əs)
scintillating ('sin tə lāt iŋ)
winsome ('win səm)

12. (adj., part.) sparkling, twinkling, exceptionally brilliant (applied to mental or personal qualities)

_____

a(n) _____ conversation

13. (adj.) extra, excess, more than is needed; wordy, repetitive; profuse, lush

_____

_____ expressions

14. (adj.) charming, attractive, pleasing (often suggesting a childlike charm and innocence)

_____

delighted by her _____ personality

15. (adj.) superior, outstanding; prominent

_____

_____ in her field

16. (n.) a model of excellence or perfection

_____

a(n) _____ of virtue

17. (adj.) prudent, shrewdly conceived and developed; artful, expedient

_____

take the most _____ course of action

18. (adj.) making a show of virtue or righteousness; hypocritically moralistic or pious

_____

offensively _____ remarks

19. (adj.) sharp, keen, penetrating (with a suggestion of decisiveness and effectiveness)

_____

offered frank and _____ criticisms

20. (adj.) dull, ordinary, lacking in distinction and originality; characteristic of prose, not poetic

_____

a theme filled with _____ ideas

21. (v.) to restate in other words; (n.) a statement that presents a given idea in new language

_____

will try to _____ those involved ideas

22. (*adj.*) marked by conspicuous or pretentious display, showy

_____

dressed in a(n) _____ manner

Completing the Sentence	*From the words for this unit, choose the one that best completes each of the following sentences. Write the word in the space given.*

1. She did her work so quietly that it took us time to realize that she was a veritable _____ of efficiency and diligence.

2. Of all the noteworthy civil rights leaders this nation has produced, none is as _____ as Dr. Martin Luther King, Jr.

3. To characterize the literary style of Edgar Allan Poe as "unique and one of a kind" is certainly _____ .

4. In most contracts there are _____ duties and obligations that must be fulfilled even though they aren't expressed in so many words.

5. Marie is not particularly pretty, but her engaging personality and charming manner make her quite _____ .

6. Since I could not bring to mind the exact words of the speech I had tried to memorize, I delivered a(n) _____ of it.

7. Until he rose to speak, the meeting had been dull, but he immediately enlivened it with his _____ wit.

8. Her new hairstyle, which softly frames the delicate features of her face, greatly _____ her beauty.

9. The fact that he had hungry children at home does not justify what he did, but it does _____ his crime.

10. Since we had been told that the new TV series was original and witty, we were disappointed by the obvious and _____ situation comedy that unfolded on our screen.

11. We resented his _____ self-assurance that he was morally superior to everyone else.

12. Detective stories seem to _____ her to such a degree that she reads virtually nothing else.

13. His normal desire for financial security was eventually distorted into a boundless _____ .

14. "Evening dress is far too _____ for such an informal occasion," I thought to myself as I tried to decide what to wear that evening.

15. The _____ of the fire bells as they echoed through the night filled our hearts with terror.

16. There are some situations in life when it is _____ to remain quiet and wait for a better opportunity to assert yourself.

17. His long nose and prominent teeth give the candidate the kind of face that cartoonists love to _____ .

18. The jury may have found him not guilty, but the "court of public opinion" will never _____ him of responsibility for the crime.

19. We observed that the trunk of the rubber tree was _____ a sticky substance.

20. How can anyone be so foolish as to develop a smoking habit when it has been proven that cigarettes are _____ to health?

21. With that one _____ comment, she brought an end to all the aimless talk and directed our attention to the real problem facing us.

22. Since the gym is _____ to the library, it is easy for me to shift from academic to athletic activities.

23. It would seem to be _____ for us not to make a public announcement of our candidacy until you are confident of the party's support.

24. With my _____ mind, how can I hope to grasp all the brilliant and subtle insights of your argument?

25. His highly technical discussion will have to be _____ if it is to be understood by most readers.

Synonyms   From the words for this unit, choose the one that is most nearly **the same** in meaning as each of the following groups of expressions. Write the word on the line given.

1. to reword, rephrase; a rendition, version   _____

2. tactful, diplomatic, judicious, circumspect   _____

3. to improve, magnify, heighten, elevate   _____

4. to perspire, secrete; to emit; to exhibit _____

5. winning, engaging, delightful, prepossessing _____

6. an exemplar, pattern, paradigm, model, good example _____

7. unnecessary, superfluous; verbose, prolix; superabundant _____

8. inferred, tacit, unspoken; unconditional _____

9. stimulating; witty, glittering, flashing _____

10. peerless, distinguished, unequaled _____

11. commonplace, matter-of-fact, pedestrian _____

12. acute, cutting, perceptive, trenchant _____

13. to acquit, exonerate, vindicate, excuse, pardon _____

14. adjacent, adjoining, next door to _____

15. a cartoon, burlesque, parody; to lampoon _____

16. self-righteous, canting, holier-than-thou _____

17. to fascinate, enchant, attract, bewitch _____

18. to moderate, mitigate, diminish, downplay _____

19. flashy, overdone, affected, flamboyant _____

20. detrimental, injurious, destructive, pernicious _____

21. a din, clamor, racket _____

22. avarice, rapacity; a craving, lust _____

Antonyms   From the words for this unit, choose the one that is most nearly **opposite** in meaning to each of the following groups of expressions. Write the word on the line given.

1. unwise, injudicious, imprudent, rash _____

2. to diminish, reduce, lessen, degrade _____

3. modest, plain, simple, demure, retiring _____

4. unattractive, unappealing, repulsive _____

5. remarkable, distinctive; poetic, inspired _____

6. succinct, terse, laconic; scarce, inadequate _____

7. to intensify, aggravate, worsen, exacerbate _____

8. dull, boring, insipid, flat, tame, vapid _____

9. to condemn, convict, incriminate, inculpate _____

10. helpful, beneficial; harmless, innocuous _____

11. contentment, satiation, gratification _____

12. explicit, express, stated, revealed _____

13. to bore to tears; to repel, put someone off _____

14. to repeat verbatim, duplicate, quote _____

15. heartfelt, sincere, humble _____

16. silence, stillness, peace and quiet _____

17. detached, apart, distant, remote _____

18. to absorb, soak up, assimilate _____

19. unknown, obscure, undistinguished, anonymous _____

Choosing the Right Word   *Encircle the **boldface** word that more satisfactorily completes each of the following sentences.*

1. It is hardly (**politic, clangorous**) for someone who hopes to win a popularity contest to go about making such brutally frank remarks.

2. He is so pleased with every aspect of himself that he seems almost to (**exude, extenuate**) self-satisfaction.

3. A good coat of paint and some attention to the lawn would greatly (**enhance, absolve**) the appearance of our bungalow.

4. My parents set up my older brother as such a (**caricature, paragon**) that I despaired of ever being able to follow in his footsteps.

5. She tried to convince me that the proposed advertisement would be "dynamic" and a "real eye-catcher," but I found it utterly (**politic, prosaic**).

6. Laura delivered her lines with such artistry and verve that she made the rather commonplace dialogue seem (**scintillating, deleterious**).

7. When he demanded that I immediately "return back" the money I owed him, I found him not merely unpleasant but (**redundant, winsome**).

8. Words about "tolerance" are empty and (**sanctimonious, contiguous**) when they come from one who has shown no concern about civil liberties.

9. Isn't it rather (**ostentatious, redundant**) to wear a Phi Beta Kappa key on a chain around your neck?

10. In the Lincoln-Douglas debates, Lincoln asked a few (**incisive, prosaic**) questions that showed up the fatal weaknesses in his opponent's position.

11. I realized I was being kept awake not by the (**paragon, clangor**) of the city traffic but by a gnawing fear that I had done the wrong thing.

12. I will try to tell the story in a balanced way, without either exaggerating or (**extenuating, exuding**) his responsibility for those sad events.

13. As long as we are (**enthralled, extenuated**) by the idea that it is possible to get something for nothing, we will not be able to come up with a sound economic program.

14. It has often been said that Dickens' most memorable characters are really (**caricatures, paragons**) of familiar types, rather than accurate portraits of human beings.

15. The aspiring salesperson stood in front of the mirror for hours, practicing a (**winsome, redundant**) smile.

16. Is it logical to conclude that because this substance has had a (**prosaic, deleterious**) effect on some test animals, it is not at all safe for human consumption?

17. He was the type of officer who expected (**prosaic, implicit**) obedience from the troops he commanded. When he gave an order, he assumed it would be carried out.

18. We rented a house fairly close to that of my parents, but I made sure that the two buildings were not (**contiguous, preeminent**).

19. The Gettysburg Address is so concise, so lucid, and so beautiful, that it would be folly to attempt to (**paraphrase, exude**) it.

20. What we do now to remedy the evils in our society will determine whether or not we are to be (**absolved, paraphrased**) of blame for the injustices of the past.

21. The rumors of "easy money" and "lush profits" to be made in the stock market aroused the (**clangor, cupidity**) of many small investors.

22. Dr. Morehouse combines, to a (**preeminent, contiguous**) degree, the skills of a great surgeon and the warm sympathy of a sensitive human being.

23. "In seeking to discredit me," I replied, "my opponent has deliberately (**caricatured, paraphrased**) my ideas, making them seem simplistic and unrealistic."

24. As he spoke to his followers, he seemed to (**exude, absolve**) an aura of hatred and fanaticism that we found utterly chilling.

Analogies   *In each of the following, encircle the item that best completes the comparison.*

1. **perceptive** is to **insight** as
   a. salient is to force
   b. specious is to intuition
   c. obtuse is to intelligence
   d. adroit is to skill

2. **dowdy** is to **appearance** as
   a. imperious is to background
   b. gauche is to behavior
   c. sedentary is to beauty
   d. debonair is to build

3. **efficacious** is to **favorable** as
   a. fortuitous is to unfavorable
   b. pernicious is to favorable
   c. deleterious is to unfavorable
   d. inimical is to favorable

4. **palpable** is to **feel** as
   a. visible is to see
   b. audible is to listen
   c. tangible is to smell
   d. edible is to taste

5. **paragon** is to **exemplary** as
   a. denizen is to extinct
   b. reprobate is to incorrigible
   c. heretic is to orthodox
   d. klutz is to politic

6. **florid** is to **complexion** as
   a. discursive is to appearance
   b. gratuitous is to bearing
   c. ornate is to style
   d. preeminent is to manner

7. **prosaic** is to **scintillating** as
   a. repetitive is to redundant
   b. culpable is to censurable
   c. arcane is to recondite
   d. homely is to winsome

8. **dunned** is to **annoyance** as
   a. absolved is to relief
   b. enthralled is to puzzlement
   c. satiated is to interest
   d. enhanced is to contentment

9. **inculcate** is to **in** as
   a. instill is to out
   b. disseminate is to in
   c. efface is to out
   d. exude is to in

10. **miser** is to **cupidity** as
    a. humanitarian is to greed
    b. stoic is to equanimity
    c. saint is to heresy
    d. curmudgeon is to valor

11. **antebellum** is to **Civil War** as
    a. antecedent is to Doomsday
    b. anterior is to Holocaust
    c. antediluvian is to Flood
    d. anticlimactic is to Creation

12. **jester** is to **motley** as
    a. shepherd is to crook
    b. soldier is to rifle
    c. tailor is to clothing
    d. ballerina is to tutu

13. **hypocrite** is to **sanctimonious** as
    a. showoff is to ostentatious
    b. glutton is to abstemious
    c. pauper is to munificent
    d. drunkard is to winsome

14. **incisive** is to **cut** as
    a. enthralling is to burn
    b. searing is to scorch
    c. corroborating is to singe
    d. procrastinating is to char

15. **bedlam** is to **raucous** as
    a. clangor is to contiguous
    b. contingent is to implicit
    c. conflagration is to sonorous
    d. chaos is to turbulent

16. **caricature** is to **drawing** as
    a. parody is to writing
    b. opera is to singing
    c. jeté is to dancing
    d. palette is to painting

17. **enhance** is to **more** as
    a. accrue is to less
    b. absolve is to more
    c. extenuate is to less
    d. quail is to more

18. **tirade** is to **invective** as
    a. paraphrase is to provocation
    b. panegyric is to praise
    c. encomium is to gist
    d. harangue is to annotation

Synonyms   *In each of the following groups, encircle the word or expression that is most nearly* **the same** *in meaning as the word in* **boldface type** *in the introductory phrase.*

1. **corroborate** a claim
   a. present   b. explain   c. deny   d. confirm

2. **exude** charm
   a. flaunt   b. emit   c. look for   d. lack

3. **efficacious** remedies
   a. standard   b. dangerous   c. possible   d. effective

4. a **recondite** report
   a. recent   b. disorganized   c. abstruse   d. succinct

5. **disseminate** the news
   a. broadcast   b. analyze   c. conceal   d. question

6. a **contingent** of troops
   a. group   b. lack   c. commander   d. movement

7. **inculcate** a desire for success
   a. belittle   b. implant   c. nullify   d. lack

8. a **deleterious** effect
   a. harmful   b. beneficial   c. undetermined   d. slight

9. a **redundant** expression
   a. original   b. trite   c. repetitious   d. meaningless

10. an **imperious** captain of industry
    a. successful   b. bankrupt   c. shrewd   d. domineering

11. **quail** at the very mention of his name
    a. smile   b. laugh   c. cower   d. sneer

12. the **gist** of the lecture
    a. purpose   b. result   c. main idea   d. full content

13. a **politic** decision
    a. prudent   b. ruthless   c. hasty   d. helpful

14. an inclination to **procrastinate**
    a. steal   b. rest   c. deceive   d. delay

15. **accentuate** the weaknesses
    a. expose   b. emphasize   c. hide   d. correct

Shades of Meaning   *Read each sentence carefully. Then encircle the item that best completes the statement below the sentence.*

"Alas! 'tis true I have gone here and there,
And made myself a motley to the view,   (2)
Gor'd mine own thoughts, sold cheap what is most dear,
Made old offenses of affections new."   (4)
        (Shakespeare, Sonnet 110, 1–4)

1. The best meaning for the word **motley** in line 2 is
   a. mixture of odd elements   c. brightly colored uniform
   b. jester   d. gaudy fabric

During our Nature Walk we tried to move through the brush and
undergrowth as silently as possible, so as not to startle the deer and
other animals from their coverts. **(2)**

2. The word **coverts** in line 3 is used to mean
a. water holes   b. herds   c. refuges   d. pastures

Though the enemy line held on the flanks, it fell back in the center, producing
a large salient, of which our commander was quick to take advantage. **(2)**

3. In line 2 the word **salient** may best be defined as
a. bulge
b. gap
c. bottleneck
d. spread

During the "Neolithic Revolution," as it is called, human beings exchanged
the highly discursive lifestyle of the hunter/gatherer for the more sedentary
one of the farmer. **(2)**

4. In line 2 the word **discursive** is used to mean
a. primitive
b. digressive
c. episodic
d. nomadic

When Hamlet sourly observes:
"Thrift, thrift, Horatio. The funeral baked meats **(2)**
did coldly furnish forth the marriage tables,"
he is essentially registering his disapproval of the fact that the funeral **(4)**
of his father and the remarriage of his mother were so contiguous.

5. The best definition for the word **contiguous** in line 5 is
a. close in size
b. related in blood
c. near in time
d. adjacent in space

Antonyms   *In each of the following groups, encircle the word or
expression that is most nearly **opposite** in meaning to
the word in **boldface type** in the introductory phrase.*

1. a **pernicious** disease
a. contagious   b. painful   c. destructive   d. harmless

2. munificent gifts
a. generous   b. stingy   c. thoughtful   d. sensible

3. extenuating circumstances
a. poor   b. aggravating   c. unexpected   d. mitigating

4. a **palpable** difference
a. careless   b. unnoticeable   c. obvious   d. significant

5. a **specious** argument
a. special   b. strange   c. valid   d. deceptive

6. satiated with murder mysteries
a. horrified   b. bored   c. angered   d. unsatisfied

7. a **florid** speech
a. unadorned   b. truthful   c. effective   d. dull

R

8. censurable acts

a. laudable   b. conscientious   c. puzzling   d. habitual

9. a **fortuitous** meeting

a. unexpected   b. chance   c. prearranged   d. longed for

10. a **dowdy** appearance

a. drab   b. ruddy   c. chic   d. conspicuous

11. a **scintillating** conversation

a. humorous   b. dull   c. taped   d. impromptu

12. the teaching of **heresy**

a. orthodoxy   b. fear   c. bravery   d. belief

Completing the Sentence   *From the following words, choose the one that best completes each of the sentences below. Write the word in the appropriate space.*

Group A

bedlam	inimical	sedentary	accrue
exude	abstemious	discursive	sanctimonious
imperious	equanimity	contiguous	enthralling

1. When the batter charged the mound after a "close-shave" pitch and both dugouts emptied onto the diamond, _____ broke loose.

2. The home movies he showed us of "Our Visit to City Hall" were not exactly the most _____ films I've ever seen.

3. I fail to see what advantages will _____ to our school from adopting the new class schedule.

4. As a trustee of the estate, I am legally and morally obliged to do nothing that will be _____ to your interests.

5. For the very reason that your job is so _____ , you should make sure to get some vigorous physical exercise every day.

Group B

quail	debonair	sear	dun
caricature	paragon	gist	enhance
cupidity	implicit	foist	denizen

1. Her brilliant success in running the campaign has _____ her reputation as a top political strategist.

2. All of us are imperfect; no one is a(n) _____ of all the virtues.

3. The paintings that they tried to _____ off on us as valuable originals have turned out to be cheap copies.

4. My opponent's description of the bill I have presented to the legislature is no more than a malicious _____ .

5. Even in old age, the movie star still managed to retain a great deal of the _____ charm that had made her so popular.

Word Families

A. On the line provided, write a **noun form** of each of the following words.

EXAMPLE: provocative — **provocation**

1. efficacious _____
2. fortuitous _____
3. gratuitous _____
4. imperious _____
5. munificent _____
6. abstemious _____
7. accentuate _____
8. dowdy _____
9. inculcate _____
10. gauche _____

B. On the line provided, write a **verb** related to each of the following words.

EXAMPLE: clangor — **clang**

1. scintillating _____
2. censurable _____
3. corroboration _____
4. dissemination _____
5. annotation _____
6. satiation _____
7. discursive _____
8. perceptive _____
9. inculcation _____
10. absolution _____
11. implicit _____
12. accrual _____
13. provocative _____
14. enhancement _____
15. enthrallment _____

R

Filling the Blanks   *Encircle the pair of words that best complete the meaning of each of the following passages.*

1. Florida Fats and the other _____ of McDuffy's Billiard Emporium seem to come from every walk of life. One is unlikely to find such a(n) _____ crew under any other roof in town.
   a. denizens . . . motley
   b. caricatures . . . abstemious
   c. paragons . . . fortuitous
   d. reprobates . . . contiguous

2. Office workers usually lead relatively _____ lives between nine and five. For that reason, many a "desk jockey" finds a weekly trip to the gym a(n) _____ way to keep fit.
   a. covert . . . gratuitous
   b. ostentatious . . . provocative
   c. sedentary . . . efficacious
   d. prosaic . . . pernicious

3. Most of the adults seemed to find Kal's Kiddie Karnival a bit of a bore, but their children were _____ . Though the grown-ups had clearly had enough halfway through the performance, the youngsters' appetites for the kind of fare that Kal served up were by no means _____ when the show was over.
   a. enhanced . . . accentuated
   b. enthralled . . . satiated
   c. seared . . . absolved
   d. exuded . . . extenuated

4. "The flamboyant plumage of the male of the species has always struck me as overly _____ ," the ornithologist observed. "By contrast, the female looks so drab and _____ in her somber browns and grays."
   a. debonair . . . censurable
   b. specious . . . gauche
   c. prosaic . . . scintillating
   d. ostentatious . . . dowdy

5. "We must take immediate steps to counteract this highly dangerous development," the new President told his advisors, "for the longer we _____ , the more _____ its effects will be."
   a. procrastinate . . . pernicious
   b. quail . . . prosaic
   c. disseminate . . . deleterious
   d. accrue . . . inimical

6. In a series of _____ attacks, chock-full of the most withering political _____ , the famous orator Demosthenes fulminated against King Philip of Macedon's nefarious efforts to curtail Greek rights and liberties.
   a. scintillating . . . heresies
   b. gratuitous . . . clangor
   c. searing . . . invective
   d. motley . . . annotations

Cumulative Review Units 1–12

Analogies *In each of the following, encircle the item that best completes the comparison.*

1. dilatory is to **procrastination** as
a. querulous is to commiseration
b. straitlaced is to dissipation
c. noncommittal is to equivocation
d. crass is to peculation

2. fortuitous is to **adventitious** as
a. egregious is to inconsequential
b. callow is to unctuous
c. cadaverous is to florid
d. recondite is to occult

3. salutary is to **deleterious** as
a. vitriolic is to acrimonious
b. abstemious is to intemperate
c. pernicious is to seditious
d. insular is to provincial

4. avarice is to **cupidity** as
a. sangfroid is to equanimity
b. innuendo is to supposition
c. annotation is to coalition
d. heresy is to penury

5. precept is to **inculcate** as
a. caveat is to enjoin
b. aspersion is to castigate
c. exhortation is to urge
d. allegation is to corroborate

6. paragon is to **epitome** as
a. novice is to denizen
b. propensity is to penchant
c. archetype is to caricature
d. interloper is to arbiter

7. satiate is to **jaded** as
a. absolve is to culpable
b. disabuse is to fatigued
c. dun is to grateful
d. whet is to stimulated

8. beneficent is to **inimical** as
a. meritorious is to censurable
b. inscrutable is to irrevocable
c. intrinsic is to implicit
d. vulnerable is to susceptible

9. bovine is to **disposition** as
a. soporific is to background
b. corpulent is to personality
c. sedentary is to lifestyle
d. sepulchral is to attitude

10. mitigate is to **extenuate** as
a. foist is to vouchsafe
b. quail is to retrench
c. relegate is to infringe
d. remonstrate is to expostulate

11. succinct is to **discursive** as
a. prosaic is to hackneyed
b. scurrilous is to nebulous
c. bombastic is to pretentious
d. incisive is to vapid

12. skinflint is to **munificent** as
a. ignoramus is to erudite
b. workaholic is to sedulous
c. showoff is to ostentatious
d. spy is to covert

13. equanimity is to **consternation** as
a. amnesty is to autonomy
b. approbation is to odium
c. stipend is to restitution
d. umbrage is to invective

14. ferment is to **agitation** as
a. clangor is to serenity
b. drivel is to effervescence
c. bedlam is to noise
d. lassitude is to petulance

15. enthrall is to **disconcert** as
a. avouch is to repudiate
b. scourge is to flout
c. resound is to reverberate
d. fetter is to shackle

16. aplomb is to **gauche** as
a. ennui is to bored
b. élan is to lackluster
c. megalomania is to grandiose
d. aura is to awkward

17. affable is to **debonair** as
a. fractious is to equitable
b. anomalous is to amorphous
c. sleazy is to dowdy
d. transient is to evanescent

18. sagacity is to **astute** as
a. wisdom is to provocative
b. prejudice is to dispassionate
c. discernment is to perceptive
d. intelligence is to efficacious

19. tyrant is to **imperious** as
a. diplomat is to brusque
b. lackey is to subservient
c. spendthrift is to austere
d. hero is to ignoble

20. sear is to **fire** as
a. scald is to steam
b. scintillate is to water
c. wheedle is to air
d. filch is to dirt

21. scholar is to **erudite** as
a. greenhorn is to callow
b. curmudgeon is to unctuous
c. orator is to bombastic
d. parent is to straitlaced

22. infer is to **surmise** as
a. blazon is to conceal
b. assuage is to intensify
c. filch is to swipe
d. fetter is to liberate

Shades of Meaning

Read each sentence carefully. Then encircle the item that best completes the statement below the sentence.

"Our feathered friend the thrush chirrups his beauteous song
Above the crocus beds, whose fragrant denizens
Lie nestled snugly in the umbrage of the pine." **(2)**
(A.E. Glug, "Alexandrines in a Country Churchyard," 5–7)

1. In line 3 the word **umbrage** most nearly means
a. branches
b. resentment
c. power
d. shade

A true child of the Marshalsea Prison, Tip Dorrit soon finds himself employment in one or another of the sleazier forms of human enterprise. **(2)**

2. The word **sleazier** in line 2 may best be defined as
a. socially lower
b. ethically meaner
c. physically thinner
d. financially cheaper

The oil spill had been so devastating that centuries, rather than years, would be needed to effect the restitution of the environments and ecologies affected, one eminent conservationist wrote. **(2)**

3. The best meaning for the word **restitution** in line 2 is
a. restoration
b. compensation
c. reimbursement
d. indemnification

"In order to protect the confidentiality of my sources," the reporter replied, "I often abate all mention of their names in the articles I write." **(2)**

4. The word **abate** in line 2 may best be defined as
a. deduct
b. nullify
c. omit
d. decrease

"Come, thick night,
And pall thee in the dunnest smoke of hell **(2)**
That my keen knife see not the wound it makes,
Nor heaven peep through the blanket of the dark **(4)**
To cry, 'Hold, hold!' "
(Shakespeare, *Macbeth*, I, V, 49–53)

5. The word **dunnest** in line 2 most nearly means
a. smelliest　　b. blackest　　c. dullest　　d. thickest

Far from fulfilling the bright promise of his early years, the hero drivels away his life by the teaspoonful in meaningless social pastimes. **(2)**

6. The best meaning for the word **drivels** in line 1 is
a. slavers   b. hastens   c. fritters   d. babytalks

Filling the Blanks   *Encircle the pair of words that best complete the meaning of each of the following sentences.*

1. "The large cache of _____ drugs we found in the suspect's possession clearly _____ the charges of smuggling that we have brought against him," the chief of detectives observed with an air of satisfaction.
a. contraband . . . corroborates   c. surreptitious . . . mitigates
b. covert . . . dissipates   d. occult . . . accentuates

2. In earlier times, people who professed views that conflicted with the official teachings of their religion were often forced to _____ their ideas publicly or face charges of _____ .
a. disavow . . . decadence   c. repudiate . . . heresy
b. abominate . . . cupidity   d. disseminate . . . perfidy

3. The lead paragraph of any newspaper article usually provides a kind of _____ of events in that it gives the reader only the most _____ features of a story in language that is as clear and concise as possible.
a. gist . . . lurid   c. caricature . . . provocative
b. archetype . . . inconsequential   d. epitome . . . salient

4. It must take a lifetime to acquire the vast _____ needed to compile the kind of scholarly notes and comments that one meets with at the foot of every page of an _____ edition of Shakespeare.
a. megalomania . . . ameliorated   c. avarice . . . expurgated
b. erudition . . . annotated   d. acculturation . . . enhanced

5. Modern scientists smile in bemusement at the faulty methodology and _____ reasoning behind the medieval alchemists' vain endeavors to _____ base metals like iron or copper into gold and silver.
a. specious . . . transmute   c. anomalous . . . debase
b. irrevocable . . . aggrandize   d. hypothetical . . . relegate

6. "The girl may not be Einstein," I remarked, "but her comments on life are often quite _____ and show that she possesses more than a mere _____ of intelligence and common sense."
a. soporific . . . aura   c. vapid . . . innuendo
b. equitable . . . aspersion   d. astute . . . modicum

Definitions *From the words in Group A and Group B following, choose the one that most nearly corresponds to each definition below. Write the word on the line at the right of the definition and in the illustrative phrase below it.*

Group A

abet (ə 'bet)
aver (ə 'vər)
blatant ('blāt ənt)
broach (brōch)
buttress ('bə trəs)
carousal (kə 'raú zəl)

collate ('kō lāt)
connoisseur (kän ə 'sər)
disconsolate (dis 'kän sə lət)
encumber (en 'kəm bər)
foment (fō 'ment)

1. (*v.*) to compare critically in order to note differences, similarities, etc.; to arrange in order for some specific purpose _____

   _____ the pages of the manuscript

2. (*v.*) to promote trouble or rebellion; to apply warm liquids to, warm _____

   attempted to _____ a riot

3. (*v.*) to encourage, assist (especially in something wrong or unworthy) _____

   aid and _____ a criminal act

4. (*v.*) to weigh down or burden (with difficulties, cares, debt, etc.); to fill up, block, hinder _____

   _____ with heavy packages

5. (*n.*) an expert; one who is well qualified to pass critical judgments, especially in one of the fine arts _____

   a(n) _____ of modern American painting

6. (*adj.*) noisy in a coarse, offensive way; obvious or conspicuous, especially in an unfavorable sense _____

   a(n) _____ hypocrite

7. (*adj.*) deeply unhappy or dejected; without hope, beyond consolation _____

   a loss that left him _____

8. (*v.*) to support, prop up, strengthen; (*n.*) a supporting structure _____

   _____ an argument

9. (*v.*) to affirm, declare confidently _____

   _____ that she would give us assistance

10. (*n.*) noisy revelry or merrymaking (often with a suggestion of heavy drinking) _____

    drowning care in a perpetual _____

11. (*v.*) to break the surface of the water, to turn sideways to the wind and waves; to bring up or begin to talk about (a subject); to announce; to pierce (a keg or cask) in order to draw off liquid; (*n.*) a spit for roasting, a tool for tapping casks _____

unwilling to _____ so touchy a subject

Group B

grisly ('griz lē)
herculean (hər 'kyü lē ən)
impassive (im 'pas iv)
inauspicious (in ô 'spish əs)
incontrovertible
  (in kän trə 'vər tə bəl)

magniloquent (mag 'nil ə kwənt)
nonplussed (nän 'pləst)
opportune (äp ər 'tün)
predilection (pred ə 'lek shən)
prolific (prō 'lif ik)
rejoinder (ri 'join dər)

12. (*adj., part.*) puzzled, not knowing what to do, at a loss _____

_____ by the sudden turn of events

13. (*adj.*) abundantly productive; abundant, profuse _____

a(n) _____ composer

14. (*adj.*) suitable or convenient for a particular purpose; occurring at an appropriate time _____

to pick a most _____ moment

15. (*adj.*) unquestionable, beyond dispute _____

a person of _____ honesty

16. (*adj.*) frightful, horrible, ghastly _____

a(n) _____ sight

17. (*n.*) a reply to a reply, especially from the defendant in a legal suit _____

no possible _____ to the criticism

18. (*n.*) a liking, preference _____

a(n) _____ for good living

19. (*adj.*) expressed in lofty or high-flown language (often in the sense of being pompous or over-elaborate) _____

a(n) _____ orator

20. (*adj.*) unfavorable, unlucky, suggesting bad luck for the future _____

a(n) _____ beginning

21. (*adj.*) showing no feeling or emotion; inanimate; motionless _____

study the judge's _____ face

22. (*adj.*) (*capital H*) relating to Hercules;
(*lowercase h*) characterized by great strength; very
hard to do in the sense of requiring unusual
strength _____

     dismayed by the _____ task ahead

Completing the Sentence	*From the words for this unit, choose the one that best completes each of the following sentences. Write the word in the space given.*

1. If the pages aren't _____ properly, they'll be out of proper sequence when our class magazine is bound.

2. I was utterly _____ when I realized that football practice and the rehearsal for the class show were at the same time.

3. Instead of _____ your notebook with masses of secondary information, why don't you just tabulate the basic facts you will need?

4. I would have enjoyed being in that student hangout if I had not been all but deafened by the _____ jukebox.

5. He is such a(n) _____ writer that his books occupy almost an entire shelf in the school library.

6. The big game had a truly _____ start for us when our star quarterback fumbled and lost the ball on the first play.

7. I know you are really disappointed at not getting that job, but don't allow yourself to feel so _____ that you won't have the energy to look for another.

8. Her argument that the city badly needed a larger day-care center was _____ by statistical charts.

9. Although we have had our disagreements, I will _____ now that she has always been scrupulously honest in her dealings with me.

10. The New Year's Eve party started off quietly enough, but it soon became a full-fledged _____ .

11. One need not be a(n) _____ of modern dance to recognize that Martha is exceptionally talented in that field.

12. Aren't you exaggerating when you suggest that the job of stock clerk calls for someone with _____ strength?

13. "When I first _____ this topic two years ago," I observed, "my ideas met with a very indifferent reception."

14. Now that you mention it, I don't think that "Sez you" was a particularly effective _____ to her trenchant and insightful criticisms of your proposal.

15. The mangled bodies of the victims told their own _____ story of what had happened.

16. The testimony of three different witnesses, all confirming the same basic facts, made the guilt of the accused _____ .

17. It would be impossible to _____ racial discord in a school where students of different backgrounds understand and respect one another.

18. I will not in any way _____ their plans to play a cruel and humiliating trick on an unoffending person.

19. I like to read all kinds of fiction, but I must confess that I have a particular _____ for historical novels.

20. When I saw the worried expression on the face of my employer, I realized that it wasn't a(n) _____ time to ask for a raise.

21. The speech he delivered was so _____ in style and tone that it seemed more suitable for a public dedication ceremony than for an informal gathering of old friends.

22. Although she remained outwardly _____ during the trial, I could sense the emotional turmoil beneath the surface.

23. She is so _____ with family obligations that she has rarely a free moment for herself.

24. The towering walls of many medieval cathedrals are prevented from falling down by huge "flying" _____ on the outside of the buildings.

25. I don't think you can really accuse the producers of _____ favoritism simply because they chose a friend for the title role.

Synonyms From the words for this unit, choose the one that is most nearly **the same** in meaning as each of the following groups of expressions. Write the word on the line given.

1. gruesome, gory, ghastly, horrible, hideous _____

2. incontestable, indisputable, indubitable _____

3. grief-stricken, inconsolable, comfortless _____

4. perplexed, baffled, stumped; flabbergasted _____

5. mighty, powerful; arduous, onerous; colossal _____

6. emotionless, stoical, unemotional; insensible _____

7. an expert, savant, pundit _____

8. timely, appropriate, suitable, felicitous _____

9. to assert, affirm, asseverate, avouch _____

10. grandiloquent, orotund, pompous, stilted _____

11. to sort out, arrange; to cross-check _____

12. to instigate, incite, stir up _____

13. to bolster, reinforce, brace, prop, shore up _____

14. flagrant, glaring, egregious; noisy _____

15. to bring up, mention; to introduce, present _____

16. an answer, reply, response, riposte, retort _____

17. unpropitious, unpromising, untimely _____

18. to weigh down, overload, burden; to hamper _____

19. a drinking bout, drunken revel, binge _____

20. fruitful, fecund, productive; profuse _____

21. to aid, assist, help, further _____

22. a partiality, preference, fondness, taste _____

Antonyms   *From the words for this unit, choose the one that is most nearly* **opposite** *in meaning to each of the following groups of expressions. Write the word on the line given.*

1. to undermine, weaken, impair _____

2. to unburden, off-load, relieve _____

3. puny, Lilliputian, bantam _____

4. debatable, dubious, open to question _____

5. a loathing, aversion, distaste _____

6. barren, unproductive, sterile; sparse _____

7. poised, confident, assured _____

8. emotional, passionate, excitable _____

9. cheerful, blithe, buoyant, jaunty _____

10. inconsequential, trifling, piddling, petty _____

11. to hamper, hinder, impede, frustrate _____

12. to quell, quash, squelch, suppress _____

13. to deny, disavow, repudiate, disclaim   _____

14. propitious, favorable   _____

15. untimely, inconvenient, inappropriate   _____

16. pleasant, delightful, attractive   _____

17. an ignoramus; a philistine, yahoo   _____

18. muted, understated, subdued; austere   _____

Choosing the Right Word   _Encircle the **boldface** word that more satisfactorily completes each of the following sentences._

1. I don't know anything about quiches and soufflés, but I'm a true (**buttress, connoisseur**) when it comes to pizza.

2. Cleaning up the old beach house seemed an almost impossible task, but she attacked it with (**herculean, disconsolate**) energies.

3. Psychologists tell us that people who seem to be unusually (**impassive, blatant**) are often the ones most likely to lose control of their emotions in times of stress.

4. I wasn't so much surprised at not getting the job as I was (**nonplussed, encumbered**) by his strange explanation that I was "overqualified."

5. Isn't it ridiculous to say that the disorder was (**fomented, collated**) by "outsiders" when we all know that it resulted from bad conditions inside the institution?

6. The speaker's inept replies to questions from the floor met with a barrage of indignant (**carousals, rejoinders**).

7. When they offered to help him, he proudly (**averred, abetted**) that he could handle the situation entirely on his own.

8. I truly felt that reality could never be as horrible as the (**prolific, grisly**) phantoms that were disturbing my dreams.

9. You will never be able to complete this hike if you (**encumber, collate**) yourself with so much "essential equipment."

10. Most voters today seem to prefer direct, unpretentious statements to the (**nonplussed, magniloquent**) style of oratory popular in the 18th century.

11. To say that Hal has a (**buttress, predilection**) for blonds is to underrate his sincere partiality toward brunettes and redheads.

12. What could be more (**disconsolate, blatant**) than the long drive home on a rainy night after we had lost the championship game by one point!

13. With tireless patience, the wily detective (**encumbered, collated**) bits and pieces of evidence until he gained an insight into how, why, and by whom the crime had been committed.

14. I like a good time as much as anyone, but I don't think that the celebration of our nation's birthday should become a rowdy (**carousal, foment**).

15. In spite of her long and (**grisly, prolific**) career, her reputation today rests entirely on one great play.

16. I know that he is wealthy and comes from a "prominent" family, but does that excuse his (**blatant, impassive**) disregard of good manners?

17. The opening of our show took place most (**inauspiciously, opportunely**) in the midst of a transit strike and a record-breaking snowstorm.

18. Dr. Slavin's original diagnosis, although questioned by several colleagues, was strongly (**buttressed, fomented**) by the results of the laboratory tests.

19. Well-meaning but misguided friends (**abetted, averred**) his plans to run away to Hollywood and "become a movie star."

20. What we need is not opinions or "educated guesses" but (**impassive, incontrovertible**) proof that can stand up under the closest examination.

21. His parents are such sensitive people that I'm not at all sure how I should (**broach, foment**) the news of his untimely death to them.

22. If you are going to wait for an occasion that seems (**opportune, grisly**) in *every* respect, then in all probability you will have to wait forever.

23. Our favorite tree, a dwarf apple, was so (**prolific, incontrovertible**) that it supplied most of the fruit we consumed that winter.

24. Although the Social Security system is admittedly imperfect, it serves as an indispensable (**buttress, predilection**) of our entire economic and social structure.

Unit 14

Definitions *From the words in Group A and Group B following, choose the one that most nearly corresponds to each definition below. Write the word on the line at the right of the definition and in the illustrative phrase below it.*

Group A

amenable (ə 'mē nə bəl)
berate (bi 'rāt)
carnage ('kär nəj)
credulous ('krej ə ləs)
criterion (krī 'tir ē ən)
    (pl., **criteria**)

deplete (di 'plēt)
expatiate (ek 'spā shē āt)
extraneous (ek 'strā nē əs)
inception (in 'sep shən)
infirmity (in 'fərm ə tē)
jejune (ji 'jün)

1. (*adj.*) lacking in nutritive value; lacking in interest or substance; immature, juvenile _____

   woefully _____ comments

2. (*adj.*) too ready to believe, easily deceived _____

   _____ customers

3. (*n.*) a weakness or ailment (physical, mental, moral, etc.) _____

   the _____ of old age

4. (*v.*) to scold sharply _____

   _____ the tardy students

5. (*v.*) to expand on, write or talk at length or in detail; to move about freely _____

   _____ on her previous suggestions

6. (*v.*) to use up as a result of spending or consumption; to diminish greatly _____

   _____ the treasury through extravagance

7. (*adj.*) coming from the outside, foreign; present but not essential, irrelevant _____

   removed the _____ substance in the solution

8. (*n.*) the beginning, start, earliest stage of some process, institution, etc. _____

   at the _____ of a new program

9. (*n.*) a rule, test; a standard for judgment or evaluation _____

   the _____ by which we judge great art

10. (*adj.*) willing to follow advice or authority, tractable, submissive; responsive; *amenable to:* liable to be held responsible for _____

    a leader who is _____ to reason

11. (*n.*) large-scale slaughter or loss of life _____

the _____ caused by the explosion

Group B

obdurate ('äb dyü rət)
ostensible (ä 'sten sə bəl)
potpourri (pō pü 'rē)
precocious (pri 'kō shəs)
providential (präv ə 'dən chəl)
sadistic (sə 'dis tik)

sententious (sen 'ten shəs)
supplicate ('səp lə kāt)
surfeit ('sər fit)
tortuous ('tôr chü əs)
turgid ('tər jid)

12. (*adj.*) winding, twisted, crooked; highly involved, complex; devious _____

a(n) _____ path up the mountain

13. (*adj.*) self-righteous, characterized by moralizing; given to use of maxims or adages; saying much in few words, pithy _____

_____ advice

14. (*adj.*) stubborn, unyielding _____

_____ in his opposition to change

15. (*n.*) a collection of diverse or miscellaneous items; a general mixture; petals mixed with spices for scent _____

a(n) _____ of suggestions

16. (*adj.*) showing unusually early development (especially in talents or mental capacity) _____

displaying a(n) _____ talent for science

17. (*adj.*) happening as though through divine intervention; characterized by good fortune _____

a(n) _____ escape from serious injury

18. (*adj.*) apparent, appearing to be true or actual; capable of being shown or exhibited _____

doubted his _____ reason for being in town

19. (*n.*) an excess or overindulgence, as in eating or drinking; causing disgust; (*v.*) to feed or supply with anything to excess _____

a(n) _____ of gossip and innuendo

20. (*adj.*) delighting in cruelty, excessively cruel _____

condemned the _____ dictator

21. (*adj.*) swollen, bloated, filled to excess; overdecorated or excessive in language _____

a(n) _____ writing style

22. (v.) to beg earnestly and humbly _____

_____ the court for mercy

Completing the Sentence

From the words for this unit, choose the one that best completes each of the following sentences. Write the word in the space given.

1. To me it seemed entirely _____ that the person whose help I most required should turn up on my doorstep at the very moment that I needed her.

2. In spite of all of our efforts to appeal to whatever human sympathies the kidnappers might have, they remained _____ .

3. Wouldn't you agree that TV has been _____ lately with sitcoms and soap operas?

4. At the very _____ of his administration, the new President announced a list of the objectives he hoped to accomplish.

5. The simple and austere prose of the Gettysburg Address stands in stark contrast to the _____ and overblown rhetoric of a great many other 19th-century orations.

6. Any child who can read at the age of four must be considered remarkably _____ .

7. One of the many benefits that I derived from my summer job in the new hospital was learning to be patient with people suffering from various types of _____ .

8. Although he announces piously how much it hurts him to punish people, I think he takes a(n) _____ pleasure in it.

9. When my stubborn younger brother proved so _____ to my request, I began to suspect that he had some special reason for wanting to please me.

10. The stream followed a(n) _____ course as it twisted through the broken countryside.

11. The more _____ you are, the easier it will be for swindlers and con artists to hoodwink you.

12. Usefulness is not the only _____ for including words in this book, but it is the primary one.

13. My last date turned out to be such an expensive affair that my funds were sadly _____ for the rest of the month.

14. Although I ask no special consideration for myself, I am not too proud to _____ on behalf of my children.

15. "How do you expect your mind to grow when you feed it solely on the _____ pap that comes out of the boob tube?" I asked him pointedly.

16. Her instructions told me exactly what I wanted to know, without a single _____ detail.

17. It is almost impossible for us to imagine the _____ that would result from an all-out war fought with nuclear weapons.

18. When I asked him why he wasn't going to the prom, he answered in his usual _____ style, "No dough, no dance!"

19. You deserve to be severely _____ for your misbehavior during such a solemn ceremony.

20. His _____ purpose in visiting me was to pay his respects, but I suspected that he intended to ask for a loan.

21. Our reading program this term is a delightful _____ of stories, essays, poetry, and drama from many different periods.

22. It's painful to have to listen to him _____ on his own virtues when I'm dying to give some fascinating details about my own life and accomplishments.

Synonyms   *From the words for this unit, choose the one that is most nearly **the same** in meaning as each of the following groups of expressions. Write the word on the line given.*

1. stubborn, obstinate, adamant, unyielding   _____

2. to plead, petition, implore, entreat   _____

3. inflated, pompous, bombastic, overblown   _____

4. a hodgepodge, mélange, farrago, medley   _____

5. brutal, vicious, inhuman, fiendish   _____

6. circuitous, serpentine, labyrinthine   _____

7. apparent, professed, purported   _____

8. fortunate, lucky, opportune   _____

9. forward, gifted, advanced   _____

10. an excess, glut; to cloy, satiate   _____

11. aphoristic, epigrammatic; moralistic   _____

12. to elaborate, enlarge, descant; to wander, roam   _____

13. an ailment, affliction, malady; a defect   _____

14. a commencement, inauguration, outset   _____

15. to chide, rebuke, reprove, reprimand   _____

16. to exhaust, empty, drain, bankrupt   _____

17. slaughter, butchery; a bloodbath, massacre   _____

18. childish, juvenile; vapid, insipid, puerile   _____

19. a yardstick, touchstone, gauge, canon   _____

20. agreeable, compliant; docile, tractable   _____

21. incidental, extrinsic; irrelevant   _____

22. gullible   _____

Antonyms   *From the words for this unit, choose the one that is most nearly* **opposite** *in meaning to each of the following groups of expressions. Write the word on the line given.*

1. to praise, compliment, pat on the back   _____

2. intrinsic; relevant, pertinent, germane   _____

3. yielding, softhearted, flexible   _____

4. masochistic; clement, humane, merciful   _____

5. direct, straight; straightforward   _____

6. unlucky; disastrous, calamitous   _____

7. real, actual, genuine, true   _____

8. a completion, conclusion, termination   _____

9. to replenish, refill, restock, resupply   _____

10. dubious, skeptical   _____

11. unresponsive, resistant; recalcitrant   _____

12. mature; stimulating   _____

13. backward, retarded, slow   _____

14. a dearth, paucity, lack   _____

15. muted, understated; unadorned, austere   _____

16. discursive, diffuse, episodic   _____

17. a homogeneous or uniform group   _____

18. to sketch roughly, adumbrate   _____

14

Choosing the Right Word   *Encircle the **boldface** word that more satisfactorily completes each of the following sentences.*

1. In a (**providential, jejune**) turn of events, the explosive situation in the area was happily defused and a major war averted.

2. His (**turgid, extraneous**) conversation, with its exaggerated adjectives and far-fetched figures of speech, made me realize once and for all the virtues of simplicity in language.

3. Although he is not given to physical maltreatment, I think there is a truly (**sadistic, precocious**) element in his willingness to humiliate people by belittling them in public.

4. I have had my (**surfeit, carnage**) of excuses and evasions; now I want action!

5. Given the kinds of tools the ancient Egyptians had to work with, the raising of the pyramids was an extraordinarily (**precocious, extraneous**) feat of engineering.

6. Although Mr. Vail (**expatiates, supplicates**) fluently on the need for a new community action program, I have yet to see him do anything to bring it about.

7. What disturbs the coach is not that Tom called the wrong play but that he refuses (**obdurately, ostensibly**) to admit that he made a mistake.

8. She tried to justify the lies she had told us, but I was unable to follow her (**tortuous, amenable**) explanation.

9. The prolonged drought has so (**depleted, berated**) the supplies in our reservoir that we may have to consider rationing water.

10. The sales manager said she would apply only one (**criterion, carnage**) to my plan for an advertising campaign: "Will it sell more mouthwash?"

11. My rules for effective writing are: "Emphasize what is essential, play down what is secondary, eliminate what is (**extraneous, turgid**)."

12. At the very (**inception, criterion**) of her career, she set the goals and adopted the basic strategy that were to guide her for many years of outstanding success.

13. You cannot dismiss everything he says as (**providential, jejune**) simply because he is young and lacks experience of the world.

14. I think the class show will be much more effective if it has a constant theme running through it, instead of being just a (**potpourri, criterion**) of songs, dances, and sketches.

15. Many students feel that Dean MacIntosh is a strict disciplinarian, but I have always found her (**amenable, turgid**) to reasonable requests.

16. Few things are more tragic than to see a great mind fall victim to a serious (**inception, infirmity**).

17. Vic is so (**sententious, credulous**) that he actually believed me when I said that I had invented an automatic composition-writing machine.

18. The (**inception, carnage**) caused on our streets and highways each year by careless driving has become a major national scandal.

19. "The Lord hath heard my (**expatiation, supplication**); the Lord will receive my prayer."—PSALMS

20. Instead of constantly (**berating, depleting**) the children, why don't you try to explain quietly and clearly how you expect them to behave?

21. In his efforts to impress moral principles on the children, he made use of (**sententious, tortuous**) formulas, such as "To be good, do good."

22. Experience revealed, somewhat to our surprise, that the candidate's (**ostensible, precocious**) reasons for running for office were also his real reasons.

Definitions   *From the words in Group A and Group B following,*
choose the one that most nearly corresponds to each
definition below. Write the word on the line at the right of
the definition and in the illustrative phrase below it.

Group A

adamant ('ad ə mənt)   **curtail** (kər 'tāl)
brouhaha ('brü hä hä)   **deference** ('def ər əns)
bulwark ('bəl wərk)   **definitive** (də 'fin ə tiv)
bumptious ('bəmp shəs)   **demeanor** (di 'mē nər)
choleric ('käl ər ik)   **enigmatic** (en ig 'mat ik)
cloy (kloi)

1. (*n.*) a confused hodgepodge of sounds, hubbub;
an uproar or commotion that goes far beyond
what is justified   _____

   when the _____ had finally subsided

2. (*v.*) to spoil or destroy an appetite by too much
indulgence, especially in sweet or rich things; to
glut, satiate   _____

   a trifle _____ to the palate

3. (*n.*) the way a person behaves, overall impression
made by comportment, manner, etc.; facial
appearance, mien   _____

   to judge a person by his or her _____

4. (*n.*) courteous yielding to the wishes and ideas of
another person; great respect marked by
submission, as to a superior   _____

   show _____ to the learned professor

5. (*adj.*) puzzling, perplexing, not easily understood,
mysterious   _____

   as _____ as the sphinx

6. (*adj.*) conclusive, final, representing the limit of
what can be done   _____

   the _____ biography of Lincoln

7. (*adj.*) offensively self-assertive; excessively and
arrogantly self-confident   _____

   a(n) _____ young chauvinist

8. (*adj.*) easily made angry, bad-tempered   _____

   a(n) _____ person

9. (*n.*) a strong defense or protection, a solid wall-like
structure for defense;
(*v.*) to provide such defense or protection   _____

   a(n) _____ against the encroachments of the sea

10. (*v.*) to cut short, bring to a halt or end sooner than expected; to reduce _____

to _____ expenses

11. (*adj.*) firm in purpose or opinion, unyielding; (*n.*) an extremely hard substance _____

_____ in their refusal to countenance the plan

Group B

forbearance (fôr 'bâr əns)
impromptu (im 'prämp tü)
mawkish ('mô kish)
mollify ('mäl ə fī)
onus ('ō nəs)
presentiment (prē 'zen tə mənt)

profligate ('präf lə gət)
remit (ri 'mit)
requisite ('rek wə zit)
sartorial (sär 'tôr ē əl)
thwart (thwôrt)

12. (*adj.*) given over to dissipation and self-indulgence, immoral; recklessly extravagant; (*n.*) a person given to self-indulgent and wild spending _____

too _____ a use of public funds

13. (*adj.*) excessively and objectionably sentimental; having a mildly sickening flavor _____

poignant without being _____

14. (*v.*) to oppose successfully; to prevent, frustrate, foil _____

determined to _____ the treacherous plan

15. (*n.*) something that is heavy or burdensome (especially an unwelcome responsibility); a stigma; blame _____

shifted the _____ to his political opponents

16. (*adj.*) needed, necessary, regarded as essential or indispensable _____

when she has the _____ funds

17. (*v.*) to soften, make gentle; to calm, allay (as an emotion); to reduce in intensity _____

_____ their anger

18. (*adj.*) of or pertaining to a tailor or his work; having to do with clothes or dress (especially men's) _____

admire his _____ splendor

19. (*n.*) a vague sense of approaching misfortune _____

a(n) _____ that her son would be in an accident

20. (*adj., adv.*) without preparation, offhand, suddenly or hastily done; (*n.*) an extemporaneous composition or remark; a minimal piece suggestive of improvisation _____

called on for some _____ remarks

21. (*n.*) tolerance and self-control (in the face of provocation), patience; the act of refraining from something, abstinence _____

showed _____ when jeered by the crowd

22. (*v.*) to send or hand in (as money), to cancel (as a penalty or punishment), forgive, pardon; to lessen, diminish; to put off, postpone, defer _____

refused to _____ the funds requested

Completing the Sentence	*From the words for this unit, choose the one that best completes each of the following sentences. Write the word in the space given.*

1. In his plaid jacket, light gray slacks, and tailored sport shirt, he was a model of _____ elegance.

2. Attached to every bill for the merchandise was a brief notice asking the customer to _____ payment promptly.

3. The candidate seems much more human and appealing when she delivers a(n) _____ speech than when she reads a prepared text.

4. The circumstances surrounding the death are so _____ that the police are not even sure that a crime was committed.

5. How can you watch those silly soap operas day after day without being _____ by their gooey sentimentality?

6. Somehow, whenever more money is needed for our club activities, the _____ of raising it always seems to fall on me.

7. At first, I was glad to see my old classmate again, but he embarrassed me with his _____ talk about "those wonderful, golden school days."

8. He was so _____ with his inheritance that he consumed in a few years the fortune it had taken his parents a lifetime to accumulate.

9. I think that the phrase "having a short fuse" aptly describes my new boss's _____ and curmudgeonly disposition.

10. I was surprised that so trivial an incident should have provoked such a fearful _____ in the popular press.

11. Of course, Mr. Wilentz was angry when I returned his car with a dented fender, but he showed _____ in not reprimanding me in front of my friends.

12. I see no point in your applying for that job when it is perfectly clear that you lack the _____ qualifications.

13. He was willing to compromise on many issues, but elimination of the "Male Only" requirements for those jobs was the one point on which he was absolutely _____ .

14. By getting the students to apologize for their thoughtless discourtesy, we _____ the anger of the elderly elevator operator.

15. Throughout the trial she maintained a(n) _____ of quiet dignity and confidence that made a favorable impression on the jury.

16. We heard that the South High fans were planning to "kidnap" our mascot before the game, and we were determined to _____ them.

17. By talking so much about your _____ that "we're going to have an accident," you are simply making me nervous and preventing me from driving properly.

18. In my opinion, this so-called "brilliant young man" is no more than a(n) _____ upstart.

19. In _____ to the wishes of the widow, the funeral services will be brief, and no eulogy will be delivered.

20. When the chairperson saw that the speakers were becoming more heated, without offering any new facts or ideas to clarify the situation, she decided to _____ the discussion period.

21. Although we must have armed forces to protect the country, the most important _____ of national security is the devotion of the people to our democratic institutions.

22. We are still looking for a(n) _____ answer to the question of whether or not our prisons can rehabilitate as well as punish.

Synonyms *From the words for this unit, choose the one that is most nearly **the same** in meaning as each of the following groups of expressions. Write the word on the line given.*

1. respect, consideration, courtesy _____

2. of or pertaining to men's clothes _____

3. puzzling, baffling, mystifying, perplexing _____

4. to return, remand; to subside, abate _____

5. sentimentalized, maudlin, mushy; nauseating _____

6. obligatory, incumbent; indispensable _____

7. prodigal, improvident, spendthrift _____

8. to glut, satiate, surfeit; to nauseate _____

9. to frustrate, foil, baffle _____

10. conduct, behavior; bearing, carriage _____

11. a foreboding, premonition, hunch _____

12. a furor, uproar, hullabaloo _____

13. a stronghold, citadel, bastion, rampart _____

14. irascible, testy, splenetic, bilious _____

15. exhaustive, authoritative _____

16. to appease, assuage, placate, pacify _____

17. obdurate, implacable, inflexible _____

18. a burden, obligation, duty; a stigma _____

19. spontaneous, on the spur of the moment _____

20. to reduce; to abbreviate, abridge, contract _____

21. restraint, patience, abstinence _____

22. pushy, forward, aggressive, obtrusive _____

Antonyms   *From the words for this unit, choose the one that is most nearly **opposite** in meaning to each of the following groups of expressions. Write the word on the line given.*

1. tentative, inconclusive _____

2. affable, genial, even-tempered _____

3. to enrage, anger; to aggravate, exacerbate _____

4. nonessential, superfluous; optional _____

5. to aid, assist, abet, further _____

6. penny-pinching, frugal, economical _____

7. lack of restraint, indulgence _____

8. contempt, disrespect, scorn, disdain _____

9. yielding, flexible, pliable _____

10. to protract, extend _____

11. unsentimental; callous, insensitive _____

12. intelligible, understandable, fathomable _____

13. to stimulate, whet _____

14. self-effacing, diffident _____

15. rehearsed, planned, prepared, premeditated _____

16. a weak point in the defense _____

17. calm, peace and quiet, lack of response _____

Choosing the Right Word *Encircle the **boldface** word that more satisfactorily completes each of the following sentences.*

1. In the face of insults and abuse, she showed the kind of (**forbearance, presentiment**) that is possible only for a very strong person.

2. Far from being (**impromptu, profligate**), all those jokes and wisecracks you hear on TV talk shows are usually prepared by professional writers and are carefully rehearsed.

3. Expressing his mystification at the Soviet Union, Churchill referred to it as a "riddle wrapped in a mystery inside a(n) (**enigma, presentiment**)."

4. The fine must be paid now, but there is a distinct possibility that it will be (**remitted, curtailed**) if your behavior during the next six months meets all of the court's requirements.

5. I am a great admirer of Dickens, but even I must admit that the death of Little Nell in *The Old Curiosity Shop* is too (**sartorial, mawkish**) to be truly effective.

6. Their efforts to win the game by a last-minute trick play were (**thwarted, remitted**) when our alert safety intercepted the deep pass.

7. His bitter anger was eventually (**mollified, thwarted**) by the effects of time and by our skillful appeals to his vanity.

8. The special privileges extended to members of the senior class have not been entirely withdrawn, but they have been sharply (**thwarted, curtailed**) for the rest of the term.

9. My sense of (**mawkish, sartorial**) correctness objects violently to wearing a striped tie with a striped shirt and a striped suit.

10. Scientific knowledge and the scientific method stand as a(n) (**bulwark, onus**) against the tides of irrationality, superstition, and wishful thinking.

11. Her unvarying sweetness, like a diet composed entirely of desserts, does become (**cloying, choleric**) after a while.

12. I came to realize that the demure little woman who never raised her voice had a will of pure (**adamant, deference**).

13. His constant blustering and (**definitive, choleric**) behavior may be no more than an unconscious attempt to conceal his lack of self-confidence.

14. Although I felt that he was wrong in his sweeping criticism, I accepted it silently in (**demeanor, deference**) to his age and professional standing.

15. Every experienced politician has seen young people who scored early successes in the political field and then rode (**adamantly, bumptiously**) to a catastrophic fall.

16. The recent (**presentiment, brouhaha**) over the choice of a host for our local beauty pageant seemed to me nothing more than a "tempest in a teapot."

17. Let us place the (**presentiment, onus**) for the defeat where it belongs— on each and every one of us!

18. We all admired her (**demeanor, presentiment**), which was dignified without any suggestion of "superiority" or "stuffiness."

19. After years of (**profligate, enigmatic**) living, he experienced a religious conversion and devoted the rest of his life to serving mankind.

20. According to psychologists, when you have an "uncanny" feeling that something is about to happen, you may unconsciously act in a way that will help the (**forbearance, presentiment**) to come true.

21. Scholastic proficiency, emotional stability, and a genuine interest in young people are the (**requisites, profligates**) for a good teacher.

22. There are so many aspects to Shakespeare, and he has so much to say to each new generation of human beings, that there is not, and will never be, a truly (**definitive, bumptious**) study of his work.

23. I am really surprised that he now shows such exaggerated (**deference, adamant**) to people whose "aristocratic" pretensions he has always regarded with contempt.

24. He delivered his speech poorly, but since he was the best dressed man on the dais that afternoon, he enjoyed a (**sartorial, profligate**) if not an oratorical triumph.

25. We are gratified to learn that the cancer from which she was suffering had begun to go into (**remission, deference**) as a result of the therapy she was undergoing.

Analogies   *In each of the following, encircle the item that best completes the comparison.*

1. **burden** is to **encumber** as
a. onus is to assist
b. presentiment is to gladden
c. infirmity is to weaken
d. predilection is to repel

2. **monkey** is to **agile** as
a. donkey is to sadistic
b. horse is to magniloquent
c. zebra is to profligate
d. mule is to obdurate

3. **skeptical** is to **doubt** as
a. disconsolate is to hope
b. credulous is to believe
c. choleric is to trust
d. jejune is to deny

4. **inanimate** is to **life** as
a. impassive is to emotion
b. incontrovertible is to talent
c. inauspicious is to money
d. impromptu is to class

5. **quandary** is to **nonplus** as
a. onus is to amuse
b. predilection is to sadden
c. enigma is to puzzle
d. brouhaha is to delight

6. **abet** is to **thwart** as
a. foment is to quell
b. aver is to avow
c. collate is to annotate
d. berate is to rebuke

7. **incontrovertible** is to **dispute** as
a. incredible is to refute
b. incalculable is to compute
c. immaculate is to pollute
d. incoherent is to salute

8. **criterion** is to **judge** as
a. gauge is to balance
b. scale is to estimate
c. yardstick is to weigh
d. ruler is to measure

9. **solace** is to **disconsolate** as
a. broach is to bumptious
b. incense is to choleric
c. budge is to adamant
d. supplicate is to clement

10. **protract** is to **curtail** as
a. aver is to affirm
b. replenish is to deplete
c. placate is to mollify
d. expatiate is to immigrate

11. **jejune** is to **unfavorable** as
a. blatant is to favorable
b. requisite is to unfavorable
c. providential is to favorable
d. precocious is to unfavorable

12. **passive** is to **act** as
a. adamant is to yield
b. credulous is to trust
c. ostensible is to appear
d. amenable is to comply

13. **opportune** is to **inauspicious** as
a. grisly is to horrible
b. providential is to calamitous
c. definitive is to conclusive
d. prolific is to abundant

14. **profligate** is to **squander** as
a. skinflint is to invest
b. debtor is to dun
c. banker is to embezzle
d. miser is to hoard

15. **cloy** is to **palate** as
a. surfeit is to demeanor
b. intrigue is to imagination
c. nauseate is to stomach
d. whet is to appetite

16. **herculean** is to **strength** as
a. titanic is to size
b. laconic is to volume
c. spartan is to wealth
d. stentorian is to length

17. **saccharine** is to **sweetness** as
a. turgid is to clarity
b. sententious is to coherence
c. tortuous is to simplicity
d. mawkish is to sentiment

18. **sartorial** is to **tailor** as
a. sacerdotal is to cobbler
b. tonsorial is to barber
c. vestigial is to couturier
d. juridical is to connoisseur

Synonyms   *In each of the following groups, encircle the word or expression that is most nearly **the same** in meaning as the word in **boldface type** in the introductory phrase.*

1. to **mollify** their anger
a. inspire   b. intensify   c. reduce   d. involve

2. a noted **connoisseur**
a. hero   b. expert   c. statesman   d. traitor

3. at the **inception** of the project
a. beginning   b. end   c. failure   d. success

4. filled with **magniloquent** phrases
a. sincere   b. accurate   c. obscure   d. high-sounding

5. a **providential** interruption
a. brief   b. fortunate   c. sudden   d. strange

6. a **brouhaha** that was soon totally forgotten
a. furor   b. setback   c. meeting   d. story

7. to **remit** a penalty
a. cancel   b. impose   c. pay   d. deplore

8. not too proud to **supplicate**
a. reply   b. beg   c. notice   d. work

9. the **disconsolate** victim
a. unexpected   b. injured   c. blameless   d. depressed

10. remain **obdurate**
a. motionless   b. unyielding   c. calm   d. indifferent

11. **nonplussed** by the attention
a. pleased   b. confused   c. irritated   d. bored

12. **surfeit** their appetite for strawberries
a. stimulate   b. deny   c. satiate   d. ridicule

13. the most **inauspicious** moment
a. decisive   b. unfavorable   c. important   d. fleeting

14. his **profligate** lifestyle
a. disciplined   b. old-fashioned   c. self-indulgent   d. intellectual

15. **extraneous** data in the report
a. clarifying   b. unrelated   c. essential   d. inaccurate

Shades of Meaning   *Read each sentence carefully. Then encircle the item that best completes the statement below the sentence.*

"They hove the wheel up just in time to save her from broaching to."   (1)
     (Richard Henry Dana, *Two Years Before the Mast*, Ch. 32)

1. The best meaning for the phrase **broaching to** in line 1 is
     a. turning sideways to the wind   c. breaking the surface of the water
     b. tapping a cask of rum   d. striking a hidden reef

"We can load up a piece of amber . . . with the greatest possible excess of
negative charge, and still it remains absolutely impassive in the presence
of a magnet." **(2)**
    (K.K. Darrow)

2. The word **impassive** in line 2 most nearly means
a. stoical
b. insensible
c. unemotional
d. motionless

As I was dusting the sideboard, I accidentally knocked against the potpourri
and spilled it all over the new rug. **(2)**

3. The word **potpourri** in line 1 may best be defined as
a. meat-and-potato stew
b. jar of mixed petals and spices
c. album of family photos
d. collection of sheet music

"He not content the shallow shore to keep
Dauntless expatiates in the boundless deep." **(2)**
    (J.H. Browne, "Beauty and Design," 102)

4. The best meaning for the word **expatiates** in line 2 is
a. descants on
b. expands on
c. roams
d. enlarges on

Try as I might, I simply could not swallow the mawkish-tasting medicine
without gagging. **(2)**

5. The term **mawkish-tasting** in line 1 most nearly means
a. insipid
b. excessively sentimental
c. nauseating
d. mushy

Antonyms   *In each of the following groups, encircle the word or
expression that is most nearly **opposite** in meaning to
the word in **boldface type** in the introductory phrase.*

1. berate the group
a. expel   b. praise   c. lecture   d. join

2. mollify the crowd
a. arouse   b. quiet   c. amuse   d. disperse

3. a **grisly** sight
a. spectacular   b. horrible   c. pleasant   d. natural

4. averred his innocence
a. proved   b. denied   c. predicted   d. proclaimed

5. an **impromptu** speech
a. prepared   b. amusing   c. spontaneous   d. praiseworthy

6. revealed their **infirmities**
a. strengths   b. intentions   c. vices   d. misconceptions

7. acted out of **deference**
a. fear   b. disrespect   c. impulse   d. reverence

R

8. definitive proof
a. critical   b. logical   c. unreliable   d. new

9. curtail the trip
a. enjoy   b. plan   c. lengthen   d. pay for

10. a **tortuous** explanation
a. tricky   b. straightforward   c. circuitous   d. bizarre

11. encumbered by cares
a. unburdened   b. sensitized   c. cautioned   d. tortured

12. to **thwart** their plans
a. facilitate   b. criticize   c. evaluate   d. consider

Completing the Sentence *From the following words, choose the one that best completes each of the sentences below. Write the word in the appropriate space.*

Group A

precocious	inanimate	criterion	collate
sartorial	connoisseur	mawkish	blatant
opportune	herculean	sententious	curtail

1. Although she has never been south of the border, she considers herself a(n) _____ of Mexican food.

2. I cannot forgive him for addressing our dinner-party hostess with such _____ discourtesy.

3. Our job is to _____ the papers that will be included in the package to be sent to every registered voter in the district.

4. The $10 birthday gift from my Aunt Mathilda in Florida could not have come at a more _____ time.

5. When I learned of my aunt's sudden death, I _____ my business trip to Utah and sped home.

Group B

carnage	ostensible	buttress	sadistic
remit	incontrovertible	prolific	potpourri
carousal	presentiment	magniloquent	thwart

1. A typical feature of Gothic architecture is the "flying _____," which strengthens the building by counteracting the thrust of the roof.

2. "If you are not fully satisfied with the product," the salesclerk said, "your payment will be _____ in full within ten days."

3. When I said good-bye, I had a strange _____ that I was fated never to see them again.

4. We all had a good time at the graduation party, but it was not by any stretch of the imagination a wild _____ .

5. The _____ reason for this visit was to see my new stereo, but I suspected that he was hoping to meet Frieda.

Word Families

A. *On the line provided, write a **noun form** of each of the following words.*

EXAMPLE: remit — **remittance** (or **remission**)

1. deplete   _____

2. impassive   _____

3. magniloquent   _____

4. opportune   _____

5. supplicate   _____

6. expatiate   _____

7. collate   _____

8. obdurate   _____

9. mawkish   _____

10. precocious   _____

11. credulous   _____

12. sadistic   _____

13. turgid   _____

14. choleric   _____

15. encumber   _____

B. *On the line provided, write a **verb** related to each of the following words.*

EXAMPLE: incontrovertible — **controvert**

1. nonplussed   _____

2. carousal   _____

3. disconsolate   _____

4. prolific   _____

5. providential   _____

6. definitive   _____

7. deference   _____

8. forbearance   _____

9. requisite   _____

10. demeanor   _____

**Filling
the Blanks**   *Encircle the pair of words that best complete the
meaning of each of the following passages.*

1. During the battle, the _____ had been horrendous. Where
the fighting had been the fiercest, the bodies were piled three deep. It
took days to complete the _____ task of burying the dead.
   a. surfeit . . . turgid   c. carnage . . . grisly
   b. brouhaha . . . herculean   d. onus . . . mawkish

2. Once our fossil-fuel reserves are exhausted, they are gone forever. For that
reason, we should try to _____ our use of these precious
resources so that they are not _____ too quickly.
   a. abet . . . nonplussed   c. remit . . . expatiated
   b. curtail . . . depleted   d. mollify . . . buttressed

3. Mozart was a(n) _____ youngster who wrote his first opera
at the age of eleven. Though he was never as _____ a
composer of theater music as some of his contemporaries, his output of
stage works was by no means negligible.
   a. precocious . . . prolific   c. credulous . . . profligate
   b. sententious . . . incontrovertible   d. enigmatic . . . blatant

4. Though one of his parents reacted to the unexpected news of his death
with a(n) _____ display of emotion, the other received it with
all the _____ and restraint of a true stoic.
   a. enigmatic . . . credulity   c. sadistic . . . deference
   b. mawkish . . . choler   d. blatant . . . impassivity

5. No matter how much protective consumer legislation we pass in order to
_____ would-be swindlers and con artists, there probably
will always be _____ people around for them to prey on.
   a. buttress . . . adamant   c. abet . . . jejune
   b. thwart . . . credulous   d. curtail . . . precocious

6. Friends hoped that the tearful _____ of the mother would
soften the king's heart toward the young reprobate, but the dour old man
_____ refused to yield to her entreaties.
   a. presentiments . . . obdurately   c. supplications . . . adamantly
   b. demeanor . . . mawkishly   d. deference . . . providentially

Analogies   *In each of the following, encircle the item that best completes the comparison.*

1. hoodwink is to **credulous** as
a. persuade is to adamant
b. touch is to callous
c. incense is to choleric
d. manage is to fractious

2. beaver is to **sedulous** as
a. sheep is to obdurate
b. cow is to imperious
c. horse is to politic
d. pig is to slovenly

3. torpid is to **lassitude** as
a. affable is to dissension
b. noncommittal is to élan
c. querulous is to approbation
d. jaded is to ennui

4. enigmatic is to **inscrutable** as
a. definitive is to redoubtable
b. dilatory is to punctilious
c. pernicious is to deleterious
d. subservient is to pretentious

5. jejune is to **substance** as
a. brusque is to brevity
b. vapid is to zest
c. provocative is to interest
d. efficacious is to effect

6. impromptu is to **improvise** as
a. bizarre is to precipitate
b. resilient is to vouchsafe
c. anomalous is to enhance
d. synthetic is to fabricate

7. adage is to **sententious** as
a. caveat is to hypothetical
b. cliché is to hackneyed
c. precept is to recondite
d. axiom is to nebulous

8. cloy is to **jaded** as
a. surfeit is to satiated
b. encumber is to absolved
c. prate is to enthralled
d. foist is to dunned

9. contretemps is to **disconcerted** as
a. hiatus is to scourged
b. dissension is to disabused
c. dilemma is to nonplussed
d. élan is to reproved

10. buttress is to **strength** as
a. reverberate is to echo
b. accentuate is to emphasis
c. expiate is to sin
d. debase is to quality

11. prodigy is to **precocious** as
a. denizen is to sanctimonious
b. arbiter is to unctuous
c. reprobate is to astute
d. insurgent is to seditious

12. berate is to **castigate** as
a. remit is to abate
b. wheedle is to deplete
c. equivocate is to procrastinate
d. broach is to elicit

13. thwart is to **expedite** as
a. contrive is to concoct
b. expostulate is to remonstrate
c. aver is to repudiate
d. surmise is to infer

14. connoisseur is to **erudite** as
a. novice is to callow
b. interloper is to querulous
c. paragon is to heinous
d. demagogue is to surreptitious

15. abstemious is to **forbear** as
a. intemperate is to peculate
b. crass is to expatiate
c. pretentious is to enjoin
d. profligate is to dissipate

16. irrevocable is to **retract** as
a. intrinsic is to resuscitate
b. incontrovertible is to impugn
c. inadvertent is to deliberate
d. irresolute is to waver

17. curtail is to **duration** as
a. aggrandize is to scope
b. desist is to range
c. ameliorate is to quality
d. retrench is to scale

18. mollify is to **assuage** as
a. blazon is to flout
b. collate is to wheedle
c. extenuate is to mitigate
d. permeate is to exude

CR

19. mawkish is to **sentiment** as
a. sleazy is to sincerity
b. grisly is to appeal
c. tortuous is to direction
d. lurid is to sensation

20. cadaverous is to **corpse** as
a. vitriolic is to cemetery
b. sepulchral is to grave
c. soporific is to funeral
d. adventitious is to coffin

Shades of Meaning   *Read each sentence carefully. Then encircle the item that best completes the statement below the sentence.*

At that memorable feast we found ourselves surrounded by enough food to assuage the hunger of even the most ravenous guest.   (2)

1. In line 2 the word **assuage** most nearly means
a. whet acutely
b. relieve moderately
c. satisfy thoroughly
d. ease slightly

For several weeks after their birth the callow young birds are completely helpless and must be fed, warmed, and protected constantly by their parents.   (2)

2. The best meaning for the word **callow** in line 1 is
a. featherless
b. numerous
c. unsophisticated
d. small

The constant rocking of the great ship made me quite squeamish for the first few days of the voyage, but I soon got used to the motion and had no further trouble with my stomach.   (2)

3. The word **squeamish** in line 1 most nearly means
a. fastidious   b. nauseous   c. priggish   d. delicate

At the announcement of the prince's birth the great guns of the castle spoke thunder and the bells of the city's churches clangored their joy.   (2)

4. The best definition for the word **clangored** in line 2 is
a. rang   b. chimed   c. tolled   d. pealed

"The bars survive the captive they enthrall."   (1)
(George Gordon, Lord Byron, *Childe Harold's Pilgrimage*)

5. The word **enthrall** in line 1 may best be defined as
a. hold responsible
b. hold captive
c. hold hostage
d. hold spellbound

"Anon comes Pyramus, sweet youth and tall
    And finds his trusty Thisbe's mantle slain;   (2)
Whereat with blade—with bloody, blameful blade—
    He bravely broached his boiling bloody breast."   (4)
(Shakespeare, *A Midsummer Night's Dream*, V, 1, 143–146)

6. The word **broached** in line 4 most nearly means
a. brought up
b. turned sideways
c. pierced
d. touched upon

142

**Filling
the Blanks**

*Encircle the pair of words that best complete the
meaning of each of the following passages.*

1. _____ of crack troops drawn from the various branches of
the armed forces were sent in to quell the riots and other disorders that a
few malcontent firebrands had managed to _____ in the
wake of the premier's assassination.
   a. Potpourris . . . exhort
   b. Contingents . . . foment
   c. Coalitions . . . simulate
   d. Modicums . . . transmute

2. In the eyes of the law, the accomplices who aid and _____
the commission of a crime are just as _____ as the actual
perpetrator, even though they may not have been present when the deed
was committed.
   a. expedite . . . nominal
   b. disavow . . . autonomous
   c. abet . . . culpable
   d. corroborate . . . scurrilous

3. An evening's fare at an old-fashioned vaudeville house consisted of a(n)
_____ of circus and nightclub acts performed by a(n)
_____ assortment of singers, dancers, comedians, and
other entertainers.
   a. aura . . . ostentatious
   b. gauntlet . . . prolific
   c. onus . . . inadvertent
   d. potpourri . . . motley

4. Some of my friends are the epitome of _____ splendor;
others always look like they've slept in their clothes. Personally, I am
neither as dapper as the first group nor as _____ as the
second.
   a. provincial . . . mawkish
   b. herculean . . . sleazy
   c. sedulous . . . vapid
   d. sartorial . . . slovenly

5. Unfortunately for the accused, there was no possible _____
to the _____ evidence of guilt that the prosecution's airtight
case laid before the jury.
   a. rejoinder . . . incontrovertible
   b. precept . . . specious
   c. addendum . . . inconsequential
   d. caveat . . . bizarre

6. The _____ fears and suspicions that had haunted his
troubled dreams like so many shapeless ghosts _____
and vanished in the strong light of day.
   a. squeamish . . . curtailed
   b. nebulous . . . dissipated
   c. amorphous . . . relegated
   d. intemperate . . . absolved

Final Mastery Test

I. Selecting Word Meanings   *In each of the following groups, encircle the word or expression that most nearly expresses the meaning of the word in* **boldface type** *in the introductory phrase.*

1. struggle for **autonomy**
a. recognition   b. honor   c. independence   d. self-respect

2. view with **approbation**
a. fear   b. distaste   c. indifference   d. approval

3. an awkward **hiatus**
a. pause   b. disagreement   c. revival   d. situation

4. filled with **lassitude**
a. eagerness   b. food   c. weariness   d. sadness

5. **permeate** the area
a. saturate   b. scour   c. destroy   d. cleanse

6. a **providential** meeting
a. chance   b. scheduled   c. brief   d. fortunate

7. a **sanctimonious** attitude
a. intense   b. spontaneous   c. genuine   d. hypocritical

8. an **amorphous** mass of old papers
a. tidy   b. surprising   c. shapeless   d. compact

9. an **aura** of respectability
a. result   b. cause   c. fear   d. atmosphere

10. wise **precepts**
a. rulers   b. followers   c. actions   d. principles

11. in the **sepulchral** gloom
a. gravelike   b. sudden   c. nocturnal   d. surrounding

12. **bizarre** findings
a. expected   b. weird   c. disconcerting   d. lucky

13. **transmute** the economic system
a. change   b. improve   c. disorganize   d. revive

14. **blazoned** on the pages of history
a. discovered   b. imprinted   c. ignored   d. explained

15. the **adulation** of the crowd
a. admiration   b. disorder   c. indifference   d. scorn

16. **disconcert** the players
a. criticize   b. replace   c. praise   d. upset

17. a **bovine** temperament
a. angry   b. fearful   c. placid   d. nervous

18. a **grandiose** scheme
a. profitable   b. extravagant   c. prudent   d. wicked

19. an act of **perfidy**
a. cowardice   b. valor   c. faith   d. treachery

20. recapitulate the lesson
a. begin   b. end   c. summarize   d. learn

21. a **motley** gathering
a. uniform   b. dull   c. diverse   d. enthusiastic

22. a **gauche** remark
a. graceless   b. clever   c. humorous   d. bitter

23. scintillating company
a. discordant   b. witty   c. international   d. dull

24. enthrall the audience
a. charm   b. horrify   c. expel   d. compensate

25. foment disagreements
a. cause   b. repress   c. take part in   d. solve

II. Antonyms   *In each of the following groups, encircle the two words that are most nearly **opposite** in meaning.*

26. a. hackneyed   b. provincial   c. novel   d. insular

27. a. unctuous   b. torpid   c. energetic   d. intellectual

28. a. adventitious   b. lenient   c. childish   d. stringent

29. a. vitriolic   b. deliberate   c. inadvertent   d. harsh

30. a. intelligible   b. contingent   c. antediluvian   d. inscrutable

31. a. salutary   b. vapid   c. pernicious   d. talkative

32. a. vicarious   b. surreptitious   c. overt   d. substitute

33. a. implicit   b. expressed   c. beneficent   d. constructive

34. a. dissension   b. gossamer   c. simple   d. agreement

35. a. fractious   b. dilatory   c. expensive   d. prompt

36. a. inimical   b. imperious   c. remarkable   d. subservient

37. a. pallid   b. florid   c. discursive   d. unkempt

38. a. paragon   b. contiguous   c. champion   d. remote

39. a. collate   b. extricate   c. embroil   d. rearrange

40. a. infirmity   b. sadistic   c. decisive   d. humane

41. a. politic   b. imprudent   c. abundant   d. resilient

42. a. remit   b. mollify   c. profligate   d. irritate

43. a. produce   b. aver   c. disavow   d. paraphrase

44. a. desist   b. intercede   c. exorcise   d. resume

45. a. legendary   b. even-tempered   c. slovenly   d. petulant

FMT

III. Word Pairs   *In the space before each pair of words, write:*

S — if the words are synonyms or near-synonyms;
O — if the words are antonyms or near-antonyms;
N — if the words are unrelated in meaning.

_____ **46.** herculean—punctilious   _____ **54.** thwart—expedite

_____ **47.** remonstrate—expostulate   _____ **55.** nominal—ostensible

_____ **48.** tenuous—palpable   _____ **56.** recondite—heinous

_____ **49.** querulous—sartorial   _____ **57.** turgid—bombastic

_____ **50.** censurable—meritorious   _____ **58.** propensity—proclivity

_____ **51.** susceptible—vulnerable   _____ **59.** opportune—inauspicious

_____ **52.** cajole—wheedle   _____ **60.** circuitous—tortuous

_____ **53.** corpulent—cadaverous

IV. Words That Describe the Presentation of Ideas   *Some words that describe the way arguments are developed and ideas are presented, in speech or writing, are listed below. Write the appropriate word on the line next to each of the following descriptive sentences.*

nebulous	innuendo	extraneous	dispassionate
specious	rejoinder	hypothetical	caveat
incontrovertible	succinct	addendum	astute
erudite	redundant	provocative	precocious

61. Your line of reasoning is fallacious, and your conclusions don't stand up under careful analysis. _____

62. The argument is so strongly backed by sound reasoning and verifiable data that it is really beyond dispute. _____

63. The ideas that emerge from the article are so vague and wispy that it is impossible to say if they are right or wrong. _____

64. She makes her point with sharpness, clarity, and economy of words. _____

65. The speaker raised a number of interesting questions that aroused the audience and led to a lively discussion. _____

66. Just before the publication of the history textbook, a special section was appended to it to cover the last election. _____

67. Rather than using something that had really happened, the speaker made up a situation out of whole cloth. _____

68. He has unnecessarily repeated the same ideas over and over again, in slightly different language. _____

69. In writing this article, the author has drawn on a vast store of learning, covering many different sciences and other specialties. _____

70. You have confused the issue by bringing in facts and ideas which have no bearing on the matter under discussion.   _____

V. Using Verbs *Verbs are the "action words" that, more than any other part of speech, make language forceful and vivid. In the space before each verb in Column A, write the letter of the item in Column B that best identifies it.*

Column A

_____ **71.** disseminate

_____ **72.** dissipate

_____ **73.** scourge

_____ **74.** transcend

_____ **75.** corroborate

_____ **76.** remonstrate

_____ **77.** infringe

_____ **78.** repudiate

_____ **79.** mitigate

_____ **80.** retrench

Column B

a. to encroach on the rights of another

b. to live self-indulgently

c. to spread far and wide

d. to achieve a glorious victory

e. to cut back, economize

f. to go beyond, surpass

g. to make less severe or painful

h. to reject, disown

i. to avoid a danger

j. to confirm the truth of

k. to offer objections or protests

l. to punish severely

VI. Word Associations *In each of the following, encircle the expression that best completes the meaning of the sentence or answers the question, with particular relation to the word in **boldface type**.*

81. A practitioner of the **occult** sciences might specialize in
a. astronomy
b. biology
c. fortune-telling
d. sociology

82. The distinguishing symptom of a person suffering from **megalomania** is
a. chronic depression
b. high blood pressure
c. delusions of grandeur
d. problem dandruff

83. Good advice to someone who is constantly being **dunned** is
a. Go home!
b. Keep your eye on the ball!
c. Don't waste fuel!
d. Pay your bills!

84. A scene of **carnage** would be most likely to occur in a
a. collection of literary essays
b. love story
c. fairy tale
d. novel about World War II

85. Taking **umbrage** would be a reasonable reaction when you are
a. complimented
b. insulted
c. rewarded
d. introduced to someone new

86. Which of the following is the best remedy for being **callow**?
a. time and experience
b. dancing lessons
c. vitamins
d. sun and surf

FMT

87. The best thing to do with an **onus** is to
   a. ride it
   b. feed it
   c. show it off to your friends
   d. try to get rid of it

88. If you receive a **noncommittal** reply to a request, you will probably be
   a. in a state of uncertainty
   b. deeply depressed
   c. overjoyed
   d. ready to fight

89. If you are suffering from **penury**, you should look for
   a. new hobbies
   b. gainful employment
   c. medical advice
   d. a better mouthwash

90. A famous literary character known for **avarice** is
   a. Ivanhoe
   b. Silas Marner
   c. David Copperfield
   d. Hester Prynne

91. Which of the following would by definition be guilty of **peculation**?
   a. a judge
   b. a coward
   c. an embezzler
   d. a philanthropist

92. It's hard to behave with **equanimity** when
   a. nothing much is happening
   b. everything seems to be going wrong
   c. you're very drowsy
   d. you have just finished a good meal

93. To describe an author as **prolific** refers to
   a. nationality
   b. the size of the author's bank account
   c. relations with critics
   d. the number of books produced

94. A person regarded as **squeamish** would probably be reluctant to
   a. visit an art museum
   b. dissect a frog in the biology lab
   c. play tennis
   d. prepare for final examinations

95. You would seek the services of a **prognosticator** if you needed
   a. a haircut
   b. an operation
   c. coaching in mathematics
   d. information about the future

96. The usual reason for **expurgating** a book is to
   a. get rid of objectionable material
   b. make it more readable
   c. translate it into a foreign language
   d. reissue it in paperback

97. Which of the following reactions would best characterize someone suffering from **ennui**?
   a. a smile
   b. a wink
   c. a yawn
   d. a grimace

98. A person who has suffered an **egregious** defeat has lost
   a. gloriously
   b. conspicuously
   c. by a close score
   d. as a result of unfair tactics

99. A person who is the **epitome** of wit
   a. uses it maliciously
   b. is actually not very witty
   c. is an ideal example of wittiness
   d. employs wit in a strange way

100. You would probably be **disconsolate** if you
   a. added all the words in this program to your active vocabulary
   b. ran across some of these words in the works of a favorite writer
   c. checked the word origins in a dictionary
   d. did poorly on this Final Mastery Test

Building with Word Roots
Units 1–3

cede, cess, ceas—to happen, yield, go

This root appears in **intercede** (page 7), literally "to go between." The word now means "to ask a favor from one person for another." Other words based on the same root are listed below.

accede	**cessation**	**decease**	**predecessor**
accessory	**concession**	**precedence**	**recession**

From the list of words above, choose the one that best corresponds to each of the brief definitions below. Write the word in the space at the right of the definition, and then in the illustrative phrase below the definition.

1. someone or something that comes before another in time, especially in an office or position (*"one who leaves before"*) _____

   take over from my _____

2. death (*"going away"*) _____

   will inherit the estate at her aunt's _____

3. priority in order, rank, or importance _____

   took _____ over less important matters

4. to give in, agree; to attain (*"to yield to"*) _____

   _____ to a request

5. an admission, anything yielded, a compromise; a franchise _____

   have a pinball _____ at the fair

6. something added, a finishing touch; a helper in a crime _____

   held by the police as a(n) _____

7. a stopping, ceasing _____

   call for the _____ of hostilities

8. a withdrawal, departure; a period of economic slump _____

   unemployed during the _____

From the list of words above, choose the one that best completes each of the following sentences. Write the word in the space provided.

1. This stern new measure will call for a(n) _____ of all economic assistance to both nations involved in the dispute.

2. In order to reach an agreement, both sides in the dispute will have to make important _____ .

3. The new gymnasium will be an essential part of the community center, not just a(n)

_____ .

4. The ultramodern office building that now occupies the site in no way resembles its

stately old _____ .

5. Provision was made for the maintenance of the family estate in the event that the

_____ of the mother occurred before that of her husband.

6. In a monarchy, the oldest son usually _____ to the throne on the death of the king.

7. The authorities declared that deliveries of such essentials as food and medical

supplies would be given _____ over all other shipments into the disaster area.

8. After four years of record-high unemployment, the economists admitted that the

_____ was more serious than they had anticipated.

Units 4–6

grad, gress—to step, walk

This root appears in **transgress** (page 44), literally "to step beyond." The word now means "to go beyond a limit or bound" or "violate a command or law." Other words based on the same root are listed below.

aggressive	**digress**	**gradient**	**regress**
congress	**egress**	**gradualism**	**retrograde**

From the list of words above, choose the one that best corresponds to each of the brief definitions below. Write the word in the space at the right of the definition, and then in the illustrative phrase below the definition.

1. to turn aside, get off the main topic (_"to step away"_) _____

_____ for a moment

2. a part of a slope going upward or downward _____

a dangerously steep _____

3. an exit; a going out (_"walking out"_) _____

block their _____

4. a policy of approaching a desired end by slight degrees _____

an advocate of _____

5. moving backward, contrary to the usual or normal order; tending toward a worse state _____

resisting their _____ tendencies

150

6. attacking, taking the first step in an attack or quarrel; energetic, forceful (*"walking toward"*)

_____

avoided _____ tactics

7. to move backward; to decline, grow worse

_____

to _____ into barbarism

8. a meeting (especially of persons or minds)

_____

invited to attend a(n) _____ of medical workers

From the list of words on page 149, choose the one that best completes each of the following sentences. Write the word in the space provided.

1. In her view, social problems in the community are too pressing to be dealt with through a policy of _____ .

2. A business concern either progresses or _____ ; it never stands still.

3. A special _____ of religious leaders from all over the world will be held in London next month.

4. We had hoped that the UN could prevent _____ nations from trampling on the rights of their neighbors.

5. After the first month of the term, I was considered an excellent math student, but then I began a(n) _____ movement that carried me to the bottom of the class.

6. The road spiralled around the mountain with a moderate _____ , making it passable even during stormy weather.

7. Since time was so limited, the moderator refused to allow the panel discussion to _____ , even for a moment, from the topic.

8. Since their property does not border the road, their neighbor's private driveway is their only means of _____ .

Units 7–9

duc, duct, duit—to lead, conduct, draw

This root appears in **conducive** (page 63), "tending to promote or assist." Other words based on the same root are listed below.

abduction	**conduit**	**ductile**	**traduce**
aqueduct	**deduce**	**induction**	**viaduct**

From the list of words on page 150, choose the one that best corresponds to each of the brief definitions below. Write the word in the space at the right of the definition, and then in the illustrative phrase below the definition.

1. capable of being drawn out into a thin wire (said of a metal); easily led or influenced (*"drawable"*) _____

a highly _____ metal

2. to slander; to speak evil of; to betray _____

a vain attempt to _____ his political opponent

3. to reach a conclusion by reasoning; to infer from a general principle or rule (*"to lead from"*) _____

_____ from the given data

4. an initiation; an introduction (*"act of leading into"*) _____

will take part in the _____ of new officers

5. a kidnapping, a carrying off of a person by force (*"act of leading away from"*) _____

found guilty of _____

6. an artificial channel (often elevated) for bringing water from a distance; a structure that supports such a channel (*"water-leader"*) _____

an ancient Roman _____

7. a channel or pipe for carrying substances long distances _____

an underground _____

8. an overpass, bridge, elevated railway or highway _____

use the _____ over the business district

From the list of words on page 150, choose the one that best completes each of the following sentences. Write the word in the space provided.

1. Take the _____ to avoid the traffic in the crowded city streets.

2. Buried deep below the city are _____ through which pass the cables and tubes that bring utilities and water into each household.

3. My supervisor's sensitive concern made my _____ into the world of business a pleasurable experience.

4. For thousands of years, people have built _____ to transport water from distant mountains to the cities.

5. The fact that copper is so _____ makes it an ideal metal for processing into electric wire.

6. The _____ of Helen by a Trojan prince led to ten years of war between the Greek states and Troy.

7. From the coldness of their greeting, I _____ immediately that they had rejected my proposals.

8. The writer claimed that, far from _____ the singer's reputation, he had simply written an objective account of her career.

Units 10–12

equa, equi, ega, iqui—equal

This root appears in **equanimity** (page 83), literally "equal-mindedness." Today this word means "composure, evenness of mind or temper." Other words based on the same root are listed below.

egalitarian	**equate**	**equilibrium**	**iniquitous**
equable	**equidistant**	**inequity**	**unequivocal**

From the list of words above, choose the one that best corresponds to each of the brief definitions below. Write the word in the space at the right of the definition, and then in the illustrative phrase below the definition.

1. clear, plain, absolute, certain _____

   a(n) _____ refusal

2. an act or situation of injustice and unfairness _____

   a society suffering from flagrant _____

3. asserting or promoting social, political, or economic equality; advocating the removal of inequalities among people _____

   _____ beliefs

4. uniform, marked by lack of noticeable or extreme variation; steady _____

   a(n) _____ climate

5. to regard or treat as equivalent; to make equal, equalize _____

   _____ kindness with politeness

6. wicked, very unjust, vicious _____

   _____ deeds

7. equally separated from a given point or location _____

   two towns _____ from St. Louis

8. balance ("*equal balance*") _____

   maintain one's _____ in a difficult situation

BWR

From the list of words on page 152, choose the one that best completes each of the following sentences. Write the word in the space provided.

1. A wise leader does not _____ disagreement with disloyalty.

2. In any just society, the persecution of racial, ethnic, or religious minorities must be condemned as _____ .

3. The evidence in favor of her innocence is so _____ that I am sure she will be acquitted.

4. The management of the company agreed to set up a committee to correct any _____ in their hiring practices.

5. Anyone who is going to be your companion on a long and exhausting backpacking trip should have not only the right physical attributes but a(n) _____ disposition as well.

6. All points on the circumference of a circle are _____ from its center.

7. The _____ principles of Lafayette led him to fight for the rights of a people thousands of miles from his homeland.

8. Will yoga exercises help me maintain my emotional _____ during periods of stress?

Units 13–15

quer, ques, quis—to seek, ask

This root appears in **requisite** (page 128), which means "essential, necessary." Other words based on the same root are listed below.

disquisition	**inquisition**	**perquisite**	**query**
inquest	**inquisitive**	**prerequisite**	**requisition**

From the list of words above, choose the one that best corresponds to each of the brief definitions below. Write the word in the space at the right of the definition, and then in the illustrative phrase below the definition.

1. an extra payment, bonus; anything received for work besides regular compensation *("that which is sought")* _____

   enjoyed the _____ of her office

2. a legal inquiry before a jury *("asking into")* _____

   attend the coroner's _____

154

3. that which is necessary beforehand; a qualification (as for enrolling in a course)

a(n) _____ for advanced Spanish

4. a long and formal speech or writing about a subject

prepared a scholarly _____

5. a severe investigation; an official inquiry conducted with little regard for human rights

turned a simple interview into a(n) _____

6. to ask, ask about, inquire into; to express doubts about; a question or inquiry

_____ the young people about their plans

7. eager for knowledge; given to inquiry or research, curious; nosy, prying

a(n) _____ mind

8. a demand or application made in an authoritative way; to demand or call for with authority

submitted a(n) _____ for ten additional trucks

From the list of words on page 153, choose the one that best completes each of the following sentences. Write the word in the space provided.

1. We can issue no supplies without a properly executed _____ .

2. The public library is prepared to answer _____ on a wide variety of subjects.

3. We objected strenuously to his questioning, which we felt had turned into a(n) _____ into our behavior.

4. Because of the suspicious circumstances surrounding her sudden death, the body was exhumed and a(n) _____ held.

5. A law degree is the minimum _____ for this job.

6. Her long _____ on the need for personal values and standards was so abstract that I found little in it that I could relate to.

7. Can you understand why she is being so _____ about matters that are really none of her concern?

8. The pay for this job is not very good, but the _____ , such as free housing and use of a car, make it attractive.

Enhancing Your Vocabulary

Units 1-3

Latin Phrases in English

As you may already know, **ex officio,** introduced on page 13, is just one of a large group of phrases that English has borrowed without change from Latin. Here are a few other such phrases to add to your active vocabulary.

alma mater
alter ego
casus belli
modus operandi (*or* **m.o.**)

persona non grata
prima facie
pro tempore (*or* **pro tem**)
status quo

From the list of phrases above, choose the item that corresponds to each of the brief definitions below. Write the phrase in the blank space provided at the right.

1. based upon a first impression, apparent; self-evident _____

   Literal Latin Meaning: "at first sight"

2. a method of working or operating, especially for a criminal _____

   Literal Latin Meaning: "a means of doing (something)"

3. the school, college, or university that a person has graduated from _____

   Literal Latin Meaning: "nourishing mother"

4. an act or development that justifies a declaration of war _____

   Literal Latin Meaning: "the cause of a war"

5. an unacceptable or unwelcome person; unwelcome _____

   Literal Latin Meaning: "a person (whose presence is) not welcome"

6. a second self, a double _____

   Literal Latin Meaning: "another I (me)"

7. temporary, for a short time _____

   Literal Latin Meaning: "for the time (being)"

8. the existing state of affairs or conditions _____

   Literal Latin Meaning: "the state in which (something is or was)"

From the list of phrases above, choose the item that best completes each of the following sentences. Write the phrase in the space provided.

1. My closest friend and I are so alike in looks, tastes, and abilities that most people consider her my _____ .

2. "That man has caused so much trouble for my family in the past few years that he is definitely _____ in our house," I said.

3. The police can often learn a great deal about a cat burglar or a bank robber by studying his or her _____ .

4. Though the Vice President officially presides over the Senate, this body may choose a President _____ to fill in for him from time to time.

5. "I thoroughly enjoyed my four years at college," I observed, "and I often return to my _____ for reunions with my classmates."

6. Though many factors were involved in the outbreak of the Civil War, the shelling of Fort Sumter in 1861 was the actual _____ .

7. The war between the two countries ended in stalemate, and the peace treaty that concluded it did nothing more than preserve the _____ prior to the outbreak of hostilities.

8. "Though a jury will have to decide the merits of the case," the district attorney said, "the _____ evidence strongly suggests that the accused is guilty.

Units 4-6

Fused Phrases The members of one group of English words were formed in a very curious way. Each is made up of a two- or three-word phrase that has been written as if it were one word. A good example of such a "fused phrase" is **sinecure,** introduced on page 44. This word is simply the Latin phrase meaning "without care" run together. Here are a few other examples of this phenomenon.

akimbo	**metaphysics**
checkmate	**orotund**
dismal	**osprey**
legerdemain	**pedestal**

From the list of words above, choose the item that corresponds to each of the brief definitions below. Write the word on the line at the right of the definition.

1. in chess, to attack an opponent's king in a way that allows no escape; to defeat completely; an utter defeat   _____

> *Origin:* "The king is dead." (Arabic)

2. a support or base for a statue or other upright structure   _____

> *Origin:* "the foot of a stall" (Italian)

3. trickery, deception, sleight of hand   _____

> *Origin:* "light of hand" (French)

4. a fish-eating hawk that has dark feathers on its back and white feathers on its stomach   _____

> *Origin:* "a bird of prey" (Latin)

5. causing gloom or depression; causing fear or dismay   _____

> *Origin:* "evil days" (Latin)

6. the branch of philosophy that investigates the nature of first
principles and problems of ultimate reality _____

> *Origin:* "the things that come after the physics (in the medieval
> arrangement of Aristotle's works)" (Greek)

7. sonorous, pompous _____

> *Origin:* "with round mouth" (Latin)

8. with hands on hips and elbows turned outwards _____

> *Origin:* probably "bent like a bow" (Old Norse)

> *From the list of words on page 156, choose the one that best
> completes each of the following sentences. Write the word in
> the space provided.*

1. Suddenly a huge _____ swooped down from the sky, skimmed
along the surface of the lake, and plucked a fish from the water.

2. Two border guards, their arms _____ , stood at the other end of
the bridge, blocking our way to freedom!

3. Magicians depend on _____ to bring off many of their tricks and
fool a suspicious audience.

4. When I was in college, I took a number of courses in logic, _____ ,
and the history of philosophy.

5. Nothing on earth can match the _____ sight of an entire city
engulfed in flames.

6. Though Caesar was reputed to be a very simple and straightforward speaker,
Cicero was known for his _____ style of delivery.

7. Even though your favorite singer has many admirable qualities, you shouldn't put
her up on a(n) _____ as if she were a goddess or a statue.

8. The game came to an abrupt end when one of the players smugly announced to
the other, "_____ in three moves!"

Units 7-9

**A Verbal
Diversion**

The appearance of **bovine** in the word list for Unit 8 (page 63)
should remind you that Modern English is rich in colloquial
expressions involving the names of members of the animal
kingdom. Two such expressions are *chicken feed* (meaning "a
woefully insufficient sum of money") and *to smell a rat*
(meaning "to suspect that something is not quite as it should
be"). A number of similar phrases, all widely used today in
informal speech and writing, are listed below.

bookworm	**red herring**
frog in one's throat	**sacred cow**
get one's goat	**shanks' mare**
go to the dogs	**white elephant**

158

From the list of expressions on page 157, choose the item that corresponds to each of the brief definitions below. Write the item in the blank space at the right of the definition and then in the illustrative phrase below it.

1. something that distracts attention from the real issue _____

drag in a _____

2. a rare and expensive possession that is a financial burden to maintain; something of dubious value that its owner no longer wants _____

nothing but a _____

3. something that cannot be criticized or meddled with _____

unwilling to confront such a _____

4. one's own legs as a means of transportation _____

arrive on _____

5. a person unusually devoted to reading or study _____

a _____ rather than an athlete

6. congestion that prevents clear speech; hoarseness _____

clear the _____

7. to deteriorate, go downhill _____

let the house _____

8. to make angry or annoyed _____

behavior that always _____

From the list of expressions on page 157, choose the item that best completes each of the following sentences. Write it in the space provided.

1. When she asked me how I got to school that morning, I told her that I had come on

_____ .

2. Every mystery writer includes one or two nice _____ in his or her stories just to throw the reader off the right track.

3. I suddenly got such a bad _____ that I had to stop in mid-sentence and cough.

4. When I was a child, I spent most of my time watching television, but now I'm a real

_____ .

5. At first, I thought I'd gotten a real bargain when I bought that secondhand car, but it has unfortunately proved to be something of a _____ .

6. "You will never be able to solve the problems facing you in the future," I said pointedly, "if you continue to regard certain matters as _____ ."

7. That part of town used to be extremely attractive, but lately it has really been

_____ .

8. Though I am perfectly willing to put up with certain kinds of behavior, others really

_____ .

Units 10-12

Place-Names in Common Use

A fair number of common English words are derived from the names of places. One such word, **bedlam,** was introduced on page 83. It is a corruption of the name of a notorious hospital and insane asylum that used to be in London, St. Mary of Bethlehem. Here are a few other words derived from place-names to add to your active vocabulary.

academy **limerick**
bunkum **mecca**
cologne **sybaritic**
donnybrook **varnish**

From the list of words above, choose the item that corresponds to each of the brief definitions below. Write the word in the space at the right of the definition.

1. a humorous or nonsensical verse form, made up of five lines usually having the rhyme scheme *aabba*. _____

   Place Involved: a county in Ireland. The name of this county was first applied to the verse form (invented by Edward Lear) towards the end of the 19th century.

2. an oil-based paint used to coat a surface with a hard, glossy finish; to give something a smooth and glossy finish; to give a deceptively attractive appearance, embellish _____

   Place Involved: probably the ancient city of Berenike in Libya, where such paints were thought to have first been used

3. a scented liquid made of alcohol and various fragrant oils _____

   Place Involved: the city in West Germany where the inventor of the product, Johann Maria Farina, settled in 1709

4. any place regarded as the center of attraction, interest, or activity _____

   Place involved: the city in western Saudi Arabia that is the focus of Muslim religious devotion because it was the birthplace of Mohammed

5. empty or meaningless talk, claptrap _____

   Place Involved: a county in North Carolina whose name was first applied to empty political speeches about 1820 by Felix Walker, a U.S. Congressman

6. a brawl, free-for-all _____

   Place Involved: the site of an annual fair near Dublin, Ireland, where such brawls were reputed to be common

7. devoted to pleasure and luxury _____

> *Place Involved:* an ancient Greek city on the Gulf of Taranto in southern Italy, famous for its luxurious lifestyle before its destruction in 519 B.C.

8. a secondary school or institution of higher learning; any place where special subjects, arts, or skills are taught; a society for the advancement of the arts and sciences _____

> *Place Involved:* the ancient Greek philospher Plato's school outside Athens

---

From the list of words on page 159, choose the item that best completes each of the following sentences. Write the word in the space provided.

1. When two players suddenly started to throw punches at each other, an ugly bench-clearing _____ ensued.

2. I learned how to ride a horse at the riding _____ that my aunt ran on her farm in Virginia.

3. The shelves on my new bookcase really began to sparkle after I applied a fresh coat of _____ to them.

4. For over an hour, the comedian entertained the audience with a string of clever _____ involving people in the public eye.

5. I found it almost impossible to believe that the austere old man I was speaking to had once led an extravagantly _____ life.

6. Over the years, San Juan's reputation as a tourist _____ and vacationer's paradise has grown by leaps and bounds.

7. The candidate's acceptance speech may have sounded impressive to others, but I thought it was just a lot of _____ .

8. "The only way he'll ever come out of this situation smelling like a rose," I observed, "is if someone spills a bottle of _____ on him!"

Units 13-15

Classical Contributions to English

The geography, history, and mythology of the classical world of Greece and Rome have contributed much to the richness and variety of Modern English. One such contribution is **herculean,** introduced on page 114. This word is derived from the name of the Greek hero Hercules, who was famous for the mighty feats or "labors" he performed. Here are a few other words and expressions of this type to add to your vocabulary.

Achilles' heel	**marathon**
as rich as Croesus	**mausoleum**
atlas	**mentor**
hector	**odyssey**
leave no stone unturned	**spartan**

EYV

From the list of expressions on page 160, choose the item that corresponds to each of the brief definitions below. Write the expression in the blank space provided at the right.

1. a long-distance race (in the modern Olympic games, a little over 26 miles)

_____

    Source: the site of the battle in which the Greeks defeated the forces of the Persian king Darius in 490 B.C. After the battle, the messenger Phidippides ran the 23 miles to Athens to announce the victory.

2. a vulnerable point, chink in one's armor

_____

    Source: the legend surrounding the death of Homer's most famous hero. When this warrior was an infant, his mother dipped him in the River Styx to make him impervious to mortal wounds. However, the part of the body by which she held him remained vulnerable because the waters of the Styx did not touch it. Consequently, the hero was killed by an arrow driven into this part of his body.

3. marked by simplicity, frugality, and the avoidance of luxury; austere

_____

    Source: the famous city-state of ancient Greece that was Athens' chief rival in the power politics of the time. The city's inhabitants were known for their frugality and self-discipline.

4. a bound collection of maps and charts

_____

    Source: the name of the Titan (Giant) who was condemned (for his part in a war against the gods) to support the world on his shoulders. Pictures showing him holding up the world were common in 16th-century books of maps.

5. a large building housing a tomb or tombs

_____

    Source: the name of a 4th-century B.C. king of Caria (a region in southwest Turkey), whose wife erected a splendid tomb at Halicarnassus to hold his remains

6. an extended wandering or journey

_____

    Source: Homer's famous epic poem recounting the adventures of Ulysses during his ten-year voyage home from the Trojan War

7. to intimidate or bully

_____

    Source: the name of the Trojan prince killed by Achilles in Homer's *Iliad.* In early drama, this prince was often portrayed as a blustering bully.

8. a wise and trusted counselor, advisor, or teacher

_____

    Source: the name of Ulysses' trusted counselor and the guardian and teacher of his son, Telemachus

9. to spare no time, effort, or expense in accomplishing something

_____

    Source: an incident in Greek history. After a battle between the Persians and the Thebans, the defeated Persian general was believed to have left behind great valuables hidden under his tent. When the victorious Theban general searched for them, however, he found nothing. In frustration, he consulted the oracle at Delphi, which gave him this advice. He followed the advice and found the treasure.

10. fabulously wealthy
           _____

> *Source:* The last king of Lydia, a region in western Turkey, had a reputation among the Greeks for being extremely wealthy, and he became the personification of limitless wealth in the Greek-speaking world.

> *From the list of expressions on page 160, choose the item that best completes each of the following sentences. Write the item in the space provided.*

1. "We are definitely committed to this project," the editor-in-chief said, "and we will

_____ in order have it ready for the opening of school next fall."

2. The wisdom and perceptiveness of the _____ who directed my doctoral thesis at the university saved me from many embarrassing mistakes.

3. I'd love to take part in one of those year-long _____ around the Pacific that Jacques Cousteau always seems to be undertaking.

4. Though the man is intelligent and informed, his inability to get on with his fellow

workers has proved to be a real _____ for him.

5. A runner in a(n) _____ depends on stamina and endurance to win a race; a sprinter relies on speed.

6. The lavish meal served at the banquet was a delightful change of pace from the

rather _____ fare I was used to.

7. When I needed to know where Kuala Lumpur was, I went to the library and looked

up the place in a(n) _____ .

8. When he realized that sweet talk and flattery was getting him nowhere, he tried to

_____ me into agreement.

9. The building was originally designed as a(n) _____ to hold the mortal remains of a Roman emperor, but it was later converted into a fort.

10. "Even though she's _____ ," I remarked, "she dresses like a pauper."

Working with Parts of Speech

Units 1–3

Nouns A noun names a person, place, thing, quality, action, or idea. For example, *soldier, kitchen, fork, hope, murder,* and *evolution* are all nouns. In Units 1–3 we encountered a number of useful nouns, including *approbation, epitome,* and *proclivity.* Here are a few more nouns you may wish to add to your active vocabulary.

avatar	**equipoise**	**mogul**	**skulduggery**
brickbat	**figurehead**	**resurgence**	**nomenclature**

From the list of words above, choose the item that corresponds to each of the brief definitions below. Write the word in the space at the right of the definition and then in the illustrative phrase below it.

1. an underhanded device or trick; devious or unscrupulous behavior _____

suspected of _____ in winning the contract

2. a state of equilibrium; a counterbalance _____

serves as a(n) _____ to the House of Representatives

3. a great, powerful, or important person, magnate _____

a Wall Street _____

4. a fragment of hard material (*e.g.,* stone) used as a missile; an uncomplimentary remark _____

hurled _____ at the offender

5. the system or set of technical terms used in a particular science, art, or trade; the act or process of naming _____

using the proper anatomical _____

6. the incarnation of a Hindu deity; an incarnation in human form; the human embodiment of a concept or philosophy; a variant form of an entity _____

the very _____ of American conservatism

7. a rising again to life, prominence, or activity, renascence _____

the _____ of Nazism in contemporary Germany

8. a statue or sculpture, often of a woman, on a ship's bow; someone who is the head of something in name only _____

restored ships' _____ for a living

From the list of words above, choose the item that best completes each of the following sentences. Write the word in the space provided.

1. With the _____ of strife between the houses of Lancaster and York in the 1460s, England once again entered a period of civil war.

2. The old saw that the monarch reigns but does not rule clearly reveals the sovereign's position as a mere _____ in the British government.

WPS

3. "Boss" Tweed's rise to prominence in New York City's government in the 1860s involved no little political _____ and backroom bargaining.

4. A number of eminent scientists — among them the great Swedish botanist Carolus Linnaeus — were instrumental in the development of the _____ for organizing and classifying the world's plant life.

5. "Fending off the verbal _____ of my opponents is all part of a long day's work," the President sighed wearily.

6. Samuel Goldwyn, Louis B. Mayer, and the other _____ of Hollywood's past have left us a rich film legacy of tears and laughter, hope and despair, triumph and tragedy.

7. Since it covers much the same ground in much the same manner, Spenser's *Faerie Queene* may justly be considered the English _____ of the Italian verse romances of Tasso and Ariosto.

8. For many months the ghastly experiences of that night and the frightful nightmares they engendered did much to upset the _____ of my otherwise placid and carefree existence.

Units 4–6

Verbs

Verbs denote actions or states of being — for example, *strike* and *become*. In Units 4–6 we encountered several useful verbs, including *infer, filch,* and *transgress.* Here are a few more verbs that you might find helpful in your daily life and schoolwork. (NOTE: Some of the words given below may also be used as nouns.)

dither	**gallivant**	**preen**	**spawn**
extrude	**parlay**	**reinstate**	**transpire**

From the list of words above, choose the item that corresponds to each of the brief definitions below. Write the word in the space at the right of the definition and then in the illustrative phrase below it.

1. to transform or enlarge into something much more valuable, exploit successfully   _____

_____ my winnings into a fortune

2. to lay eggs or produce young, especially in great numbers; to bring forth or generate   _____

the streams in which the salmon _____

3. to shiver or tremble; to act in a highly nervous, excited, but indecisive way, vacillate   _____

_____ endlessly in a crisis

4. to give off a fluid or vapor through pores or the like; to come to light, be revealed; to occur   _____

what _____ during the trial

5. (*of a bird*) to trim or dress with the beak; to make oneself smooth or sleek, primp; to pride oneself on, gloat over

_____ before the mirror

6. to push, force, or press out; to shape by forcing through a die or mold

lava that has been _____ by a volcano

7. to restore to a former possession or position

_____ the excised paragraph

8. to go about in an ostentatious or indiscreet manner with members of the opposite sex; to move or roam about seeking pleasure; generally to move, go, travel

_____ about town at all hours of night

From the list of words on page 164, choose the item that best completes each of the following sentences. Write the word in the space provided.

1. It is a well-known scientific fact that a plant _____ more fully on a dry, hot day than it does on a cold, wet one.

2. Some years after he had been driven from office by a military coup, the duly elected president was _____ with American aid.

3. "Education is the only way we will eradicate ignorance," the speaker declared, "and the prejudice and misunderstanding it _____ ."

4. During the first three acts of Shakespeare's great tragedy, the villainous Richard III, step by nefarious step, _____ his claims to the throne into a crown.

5. If she had a fault, it was a propensity to _____ when prompt and decisive action was required.

6. My kids love to watch the motor on my home pasta machine _____ individual strands of spaghetti through the perforated nozzle on the front.

7. As far as I could see, my "fabulous (albeit expensive) talking parrot" did nothing but _____ its feathers and eat me out of house and home.

8. On that cozy winter evening the flames in the fire crackled cheerfully as the smoke _____ merrily up the chimney.

Units 7–9

Adjectives

An *adjective* describes or qualifies a noun. Among the adjectives we encountered in Units 7–9 were *punctilious, acrimonious,* and *slovenly.* Here are a few more adjectives that you may wish to add to your active vocabulary. (NOTE: Two of the words can also be used as nouns.)

cavalier	heuristic	immemorial	raffish	ulterior
elliptical	hortatory	proprietary	symbiotic	untoward

From the list of words on page 165, choose the item that corresponds to each of the brief definitions below. Write the word in the space at the right of the definition and then in the illustrative phrase below it.

1. living together in close union or in a mutually beneficial relationship; mutual, cooperative; parasitic _____

_____ living arrangements

2. existing from beyond the reach of written record, human memory, or tradition _____

from time _____

3. shaped like an ellipse; marked by sudden, abrupt leaps from one topic to another; characterized by extreme economy of words, speech, or writing, deliberately obscure or convoluted _____

an extremely _____ argument

4. difficult to guide or manage, unruly, intractable; marked by trouble or unhappiness, unlucky; not favorable, adverse, unpropitious; not proper or decorous _____

_____ developments

5. serving as an aid to learning or discovery by means of trial-and-error methods; utilizing exploratory self-education techniques to improve performance _____

a(n) _____ approach

6. relating to or characteristic of an owner; manufactured or marketed by someone with an exclusive patent; privately owned and operated for profit _____

_____ rights

7. (*capital C*) relating to the party that supported King Charles I in the English Civil Wars of the 17th century; relating to certain English poets of the 17th century; (*lowercase c*) aristocratic; characterized by or given to offhand and disdainful dismissal of important matters _____

the _____ Parliament

8. more distant or remote; future; going beyond what is openly said or shown, especially if not proper or respectable _____

_____ motives

9. vulgarly flashy or crude; unconventionally careless, rakish _____

the snidely _____ angle of his hat

10. full of advice, warnings, and other commands or admonitions _____

Chesterfield's more _____ epistles

From the list of words on page 165, choose the word that best completes each of the following sentences. Write the word in the space provided.

1. In nature we find many _____ relationships, such as those between the elephant and the tickbird and between the shark and the pilot fish.

2. In Latin the _____ subjunctive is used in the first person to express a command or exhortation; for example, "*Let us go* to Rome."

3. Rabelais's prose style in *Gargantua* and *Pantagruel* is sometimes so _____ that it is difficult to determine what is being said and who is doing the talking.

4. "What is man's life," the preacher asks, "compared with the _____ hills?" and he answers, "Man's life is soon snuffed out, but the hills endure forever."

5. Occasionally, the Food and Drug Administration will not allow a medicine to be marketed because it produces _____ side effects in humans.

6. "Someone who hasn't a penny to spare cannot afford to be _____ in money matters," she observed.

7. His strange words and actions that afternoon clearly revealed that he had some _____ design in mind, but try as I might, I could not fathom it.

8. Though the author disclaimed any _____ interest in the book she'd written, she advised me to fire anyone who changed a word of it.

9. For years he lived in one of the more gamy districts of London, full of gaudy taverns and _____ eateries.

10. Since the program actually improves a student's performance on the computer it is designed for, it is an excellent _____ tool.

Units 10–12

Nouns

Nouns are subdivided into *common nouns,* naming something general (for example, *country*), and *proper nouns,* naming something particular (for example, *United States of America*). The nouns presented in VOCABULARY WORKSHOP are almost exclusively common nouns. Among those we encountered in Units 10–12 is *bedlam,* which derives from a proper noun, the hospital of Saint Mary of Bethlehem. Here are a few more useful common nouns for your active vocabulary.

cachet	inroad	protagonist	spate	vantage
humbug	oligarchy	rhetoric	upshot	

From the list of words above, choose the item that corresponds to each of the brief definitions below. Write the word in the space at the right of the definition and then in the illustrative phrase below it.

1. the final result or outcome _____

the _____ of our discussions

2. something designed to deceive or mislead; imposture; a false or deceptive person; an attitude of deception; nonsense, drivel _____

   "Bah! _____ !"

3. the art or study of speaking or writing effectively; skill in the effective use of language; insincere or overblown language _____

   a telling use of _____

4. government by a small clique of people, especially for corrupt or selfish purposes; any organization under the control of a few, select persons _____

   Athens under the _____

5. a position giving a person a strategic plus, commanding perspective, or comprehensive view _____

   from the _____ of the crow's nest

6. a seal used as a mark of official approval; any indication of official approval; a feature or characteristic conferring great prestige; prestige itself _____

   doesn't have the _____ it used to have

7. the chief character in a play, novel, or story; the leading actor or participant in a real event; the leader or champion of a cause _____

   the _____ in *The Scarlet Letter*

8. a freshet or flood; a large number or great amount; a sudden or stormy rush or outburst _____

   an unexpected _____ of anger

9. a sudden hostile raid or incursion; (*plural*) an advance or penetration, often at the expense of someone or something else _____

   made _____ into my pocketbook

From the list of words on page 167, choose the item that best completes each of the following sentences. Write the word in the space provided.

1. Far from playing the neutral observer, the newscaster took up the cudgels and became a major _____ in the struggle.

2. The book recounts in delightful detail the story of the Piltdown man and other archaeological _____ .

3. Despite its designation as a republic, 18th-century Venice was ruled by a tiny aristocratic _____ headed up by the doge.

4. The simple, heartfelt, dignified language of Lincoln's Gettysburg Address is much more moving than the grandiloquent _____ of Everett's oration on the same occasion.

5. The police beefed up foot patrols in our neighborhood after a particularly horrendous _____ of late-night muggings.

6. We can certainly appreciate the general's mistakes on that memorable day from the comfortable _____ of the armchair in our library, but whether we could have avoided them in the heat of battle is quite another matter.

7. The disease had made such deep _____ into her overall health that she was not expected to live more than a few days longer.

8. The evidence was so contradictory and circumstantial that it was doubtful what the _____ of a jury trial would be.

9. Few of the teaching staff had ever actually plowed through those dreary tomes, but those who did acquired a certain _____ at faculty cocktail parties.

Units 13–15

Verbs

Verbs can be divided into those that take an object (*transitive verbs*) and those that do not (*intransitive verbs.*) Among the verbs we encountered in Units 13–15 were *foment,* a transitive verb, and *expatiate,* an intransitive verb. Here are a few more such verbs to add to your active vocabulary.

assay	cadge	galvanize	ossify	skew
belie	extrapolate	impound	propagate	stanch

From the list of words above, choose the item that corresponds to each of the brief definitions below. Write the word in the space at the right of the definition and then in the illustrative phrase below it.

1. (*trans.*) to check or stop the flow of something, especially blood from a wound; to check or stop something in its course; to make watertight, stop up   _____

_____ her tears

2. (*trans.*) to pass electric current through in order to stimulate; to stimulate or excite as if by electric shock; to coat with zinc; (*intrans.*) to react as if stimulated by an electric shock   _____

_____ public opinion

3. (*trans.*) to shut up, confine; to seize and hold in custody, take possession of   _____

_____ evidence

4. (*trans.*) to analyze ore for its components, especially if they are precious (gold or silver); to judge the worth of, estimate   _____

_____ specimens of moon rock

5. (*trans.*) to turn into bone; to make rigidly conventional and opposed to change; (*intrans.*) to become bone; to become hardened and conventional   _____

after the cartilage had _____

6. (*trans.*) to beg, obtain by begging; to sponge off   _____

_____ change on the street corner

7. (*trans.*) to cause to reproduce or increase; to cause to spread out and extend; to foster greater knowledge of or belief in, publicize; to transmit sound or light through a medium; (*intrans.*) to multiply; to increase or extend; (*of sound, etc.*) to travel through space or some other medium _____

a species that _____ asexually

8. (*trans.*) to tell lies about, misrepresent; to give a false impression of; to show something to be false or wrong; to contradict, run counter to; to disguise _____

actions that _____ one's statements

9. (*trans.*) to make, cut, or set on the bias; to distort; (*intrans.*) to take an oblique course _____

_____ the statistics in the company's favor

10. (*trans.*) to infer an unknown value from a known one; to project or expand known data or experience into an unknown area; to predict by projecting past experience on the future; to draw out, amplify _____

_____ present market trends to predict the future

From the list of words on page 169, choose the item that best completes each of the following sentences. Write the word in the space provided.

1. Several senators said they would not vote for the tax-relief bill because they felt it was _____ disproportionately in favor of cuts for the wealthy.

2. The aura of rural peace in which the village was bathed _____ the community's essentially industrial role in the local economy.

3. "No one with your talent for _____ a free meal from a chance passerby will ever go hungry," I observed in amusement.

4. I thought it was exceedingly mean-spirited of him to _____ a generalized negative assessment of our leader's efforts from one or two tiny unpleasant personal experiences.

5. As soon as they heard that an enemy had invaded their country, the citizenry _____ into action, taking up arms and rushing to the area under attack.

6. It is not unusual for makeshift living arrangements to _____ over hundreds of years into rigid social conventions.

7. Recently the federal government has beefed up its customs personnel in an effort to _____ the flow of illegal aliens across our borders.

8. Denounced as a traitor to the "people," the famous poet was summarily arrested, and his private papers were _____ .

9. In one of James A. Michener's massive novels, a 19th-century evangelical minister travels halfway around the world to _____ the Christian faith among the "heathen" inhabitants of a lush tropical paradise.

10. "Since the life of a sparrow is a unique gift of nature," she replied, "who amongst us is qualified to _____ its true worth?"

Index

The following tabulation lists all the basic words taught in the various units of this workbook, as well as those introduced in the *Vocabulary of Vocabulary, Building with Word Roots, Enhancing Your Vocabulary,* and *Working with Parts of Speech* sections. The number after each item indicates the page on which it is introduced, but the word may also appear in exercises on later pages.